The Complete Guide to Mentoring

DISCARD

The Complete Guide to Mentoring

How to design, implement and evaluate effective mentoring

HILARIE OWEN

KoganPage

LONDON PHILADELPHIA NEW DELHI

First published in Great Britain and the United States in 2011 by Kogan Page Limited

120 Pentonville Road	1518 Walnut Street, Suite 1100	4737/23 Ansari Road
London N1 9JN	Philadelphia PA 19102	Daryaganj
United Kingdom	USA	New Delhi 110002
www.koganpage.com		India

© Hilarie Owen, 2011

The right of Hilarie Owen to be identified as the author of this work has been asserted by her in accordance with the Copyright, Designs and Patents Act 1988.

ISBN   978 0 7494 6114 0
E-ISBN   978 0 7494 6115 7

British Library Cataloguing-in-Publication Data

A CIP record for this book is available from the British Library.

Library of Congress Cataloging-in-Publication Data

Owen, Hilarie.
    The complete guide to mentoring : how to design, implement and evaluate effective mentoring programmes / Hilarie Owen.
        p. cm.
    ISBN 978-0-7494-6114-0 – ISBN 978-0-7494-6115-7 (ebk)   1. Mentoring in business. 2. Career development.   3. Mentoring.   I. Title.
    HF5385.O94 2011
    658.3′124–dc23
                                                                                                    2011019232

Typeset by Graphicraft Limited, Hong Kong
Printed and bound in India by Replika Press Pvt Ltd

Contents

Foreword

Any book that addresses mentoring in an insightful way inevitably explores the concept of wisdom. Effective mentors are almost always wise people – worldly wise and personally wise. They have great experience, but more importantly, they have reflected upon that experience and used it to understand both themselves and how they relate to the world around them. In the context of Robert Kegan's typology of adult maturity, they are at the highest level. Since only a small percentage of adults achieve such maturity, good mentors are a relatively scarce and invaluable resource.

However, the role of a mentor is not to offload their wisdom onto someone less experienced. Rather, it is to help that person develop the mindsets, ways of thinking and personal insight to create their own wisdom. Becoming wise is a process of integrating experience and reflection for greater understanding. It's a critical skill for making better career choices, for recognizing where and how to build on personal strengths and aptitudes, for developing powerful and pragmatic coping strategies to manage weaknesses, and to make better decisions more generally.

Yet wisdom is not directly correlated with age. It's said, with some justification, that there is no fool like an old fool. Like respect, wisdom has to be earned, yet anyone above their mid-teens, who has a well-developed 'theory of mind' can earn it. Some of the most effective mentors I have encountered have been young professionals and even young people still at school. The old do not have a monopoly on wisdom.

That's one good reason why I see mentoring as a life-long cascade, in which people may be mentor or mentee, or both simultaneously, at transition points in their lives and careers. There are so many of these transition points or situations – starting a new school, being bullied at school, falling behind academically, becoming a teenage parent, becoming a young person at risk, coming out of prison and wanting to go straight, leaving home and going to university, starting your first job, achieving your first supervisory role, returning to work after maternity leave and so on, all the way into retirement and the third age. Anyone who cares about other people has a great deal to offer, if they are prepared to reflect on and use their experience in these transitions, to help other people.

Increasingly, we are seeing a shift to different forms of mentoring, using different technologies and especially e-mail. Multimedia mentoring, using face-to-face meetings alongside e-mail, telephone and even texting, is emerging as a powerful way to harness every opportunity to help. At the same time, I observe what we have come to describe as second-wave mentoring – a recognition by companies and community organizations, which have been using mentoring programmes for some time, that they can achieve much more through absorbing global good practice. The International Standards for Mentoring Programmes in Employment provide a useful platform for this movement.

I commend this book for its pragmatic approach to many of the core issues and applications of mentoring – and for its store of wisdom.

Dr David Clutterbuck

Acknowledgements

Writing the book I have been given access to people in a variety of organizations who have shared their mentoring experiences. I would like to thank them for their openness and enlightenment. In Germany, I would like to thank the people I spoke to at Zurich Insurance, especially Hajo Bruggemann. From the UK I'd like to thank inspiring Head Teacher Jan Buckland, Peninah Thomson of Praesta, and police officers and staff from Gloucestershire Constabulary.

I would also like to thank my publishing editors Hannah and Matthew from Kogan Page for their encouragement and support.

This is our purpose: to make as meaningful as possible this life that has been bestowed upon us... to live in such a way that we may be proud of ourselves, to act in such a way that some part of us lives on.

OSWALD SPENGLER, PHILOSOPHER

Chapter One
Introduction to
mentoring

The Complete Guide to Mentoring is a toolkit for all those who are looking to find out more about mentoring, whether you are seeking a mentor, want to be a mentor or, in particular, you are interested in setting up an in-house mentoring programme.

For the last decade much has been written about coaching and there are many individuals today who offer their coaching services. Here, the focus is on mentoring, a topic that is even more relevant today.

Why is mentoring needed today?

We live in a very fast-changing world with chaotic and unexpected events. One of these was the global financial crisis that will have long-term financial repercussions for private and public organizations as well as individuals. To deal with and flourish in today's world, what is needed at individual, team and organizational levels is wisdom and judgement that goes beyond processes and policies. Our future depends on the wisdom and judgement of our society.

Wisdom is attained through life experience if a person has the ability to learn from experience. Extracting insight from experience is an ability much needed in business and government because working professionals so often have to face uncertainty and complexity on a daily basis for which there is no practical guidebook. Instead, decision makers have to rely on judgement.

Wisdom, at individual and organizational levels, is made up of curiosity and willingness to learn about one's environment. It is through questioning and challenging the assumptions that we take for granted that different worldviews and perspectives enable us to gain wisdom. In other words, we grow as individuals through engaging with the world, changing and being changed by it. But there is a danger – a cliff we are heading towards. Different people call it different things: an ecological cliff; an over-population cliff; an obese cliff; a fundamentalism cliff; or a banking and financial cliff. Someone who has had to explore why we are all walking towards the cliff is a senior officer at the United Nations. He concluded at a conference:

> I've dealt with many different problems around the world, and I've concluded that there's only one real problem: over the past one hundred years, the power that technology has given us has grown beyond anyone's wildest imagination, but our wisdom has not. If the gap between our power and our wisdom is not redressed soon, I don't have much hope for our prospects.
>
> (Senge *et al*, 2005: 187)

Organizations recruit graduates hoping they will be the leaders of tomorrow but studies show there is a skills gap that needs addressing. One of the studies by consulting firm Booz Allen Hamilton found that business graduates including MBA students are better than other graduates at: action, goal-setting, information analysis, information gathering, quantitative skills, theory and technology. However, these graduates were critically poor at helping others, using initiative, leadership, problem solving, relationships and sense making. In addition, almost three-quarters of female students on MBAs said the course forced them to become someone other than themselves to survive and succeed. Therefore, how relevant is an MBA today?

Is business education a factor in the business scandals of the last ten years? Booz and Company describe what business schools have been teaching as a 'rules-plus-analytics' model. They explain the model applies to the rules governing corporate behaviour as constraints to be overcome and analytical tools to work within or around these rules for the purpose of winning. Booz and Company ague: 'This model emphasises impersonal aggressiveness in which managers walk as close to the legal and ethical line as possible – even crossing over it when they expect they won't get caught' (Booz and Company, 2008).

In addition, they suggest, it is often only when the performance of a group of employees is not meeting the expectations of the senior executives that serious attention is given to learning and development in their strategic planning. This is no longer sufficient.

Today, we need individual and organizational wisdom, judgement, leadership and responsibility to move forward, progress and learn from the past. This is why we need mentoring in organizations today. An overconfident person or organization assumes stability, whereas wisdom assumes complexity. Mentoring is a powerful process for making sustainable progress based on the positive partnership of two people. It can be used for a multitude of reasons:

- preparing to take up a new role;
- support for the first year as a school head;
- as part of graduate or high potential development schemes;
- succession planning;
- as part of addressing diversity;
- support for business owners;
- developing the top team.

The purpose of this book is to share the experience of others and provide a practical toolkit for those interested in mentoring as a way to progress. This includes providing specific guidelines for assessing the need for such an initiative in an organization as well as designing and implementing it.

Mentoring can begin in school, and using a mentor has helped many young people. There is a difference between a parent giving advice and an external mentor guiding a young person. To begin with, the young person tends to listen to someone who doesn't have authority over them. At the same time, a mentor can be objective and not emotionally attached to the young person.

Likewise, in the workplace, a person is often more likely to listen to a mentor who is not their line manager and feel they can be more open and honest with someone who isn't so close to them. Mentoring can help career development and succession planning. This in itself is going to be vital over the next five years as the vast number of 'baby boomers' leave organizations, taking with them knowledge, technical skills, understanding of organizational culture and politics, experience and sometimes wisdom, leaving fewer people to replace them.

Another reason for having a mentor is when a person takes on a new role or challenge and has to get to grips with the reality and deal with the problems very quickly. They need support, just as we all do, especially when the challenges are mammoth.

Therefore, mentoring is an effective way to develop talent in organizations. It is an effective way to address the issue of succession planning. Mentoring supports and supplements other learning and development initiatives. During the process both mentor and mentee learn and grow. Mentoring addresses gender and diversity issues with proof that women with mentors move up the organization more quickly. Finally, mentoring is a very cost-effective way of developing people with no room hire, no cost of a trainer or outside consultant and no excessive time off.

In fact, mentoring:

- is a very powerful way of helping people make significant personal transitions;
- addresses current issues for the individual learner;
- supports self-development and career management;
- develops two people for the price of one!

A real example

About eight years ago a local authority decided to set up a mentoring scheme for head teachers. A list of possible mentors was compiled to mentor new head teachers. One of these mentors was an experienced head called Jan. She had worked as a head teacher in three different schools over 16 years, had worked as a remodelling consultant (a national scheme), had been an OFSTED inspector and was now back working as a head teacher. Therefore Jan felt she had the experience to act as a mentor to new head teachers. Here she describes her role as a mentor.

> I met up with a new head who was in her first headship and didn't know where to start. There was a huge list of things to do and at my first meeting, what I thought would take a couple of hours took a whole day! We developed a priority list that included easy things as well as more challenging tasks that would make a real difference to the school. I had to ask lots of questions to help her re-prioritize. I won't tell but ask questions to get the mentee to try and see the wood for the trees.

I asked Jan, who has since mentored several new head teachers, how she goes about it. She explained:

> I first go to the school and walk and talk the school to understand the context; this enables me to see where they want to go. Very often a head teacher will know where they want to go but not how to get there. In the example above, I took her out to lunch for our second session to reflect from a distance.

Getting away and having time to reflect is an important part of mentoring and something we will look at in more depth later. Here it is clear that the ability to reflect on the mentee's issue enables them to construct action to resolve it. Throughout the book there is an opportunity at the end of each chapter to reflect, ask deep questions, question assumptions and construct actions as a result of that reflection.

Jan continued to describe what she thought mentees are looking for:

> They want a 'critical friend'. Being a head teacher can be a lonely job and as a new head you are not sure where loyalties lie. That's why you need an experienced head or someone who is in their second year as a head teacher and can remember their first year experience. Sometimes the challenges are so great that a mentor needs to be someone who has been a head several times.

I asked Jan what she gains from being a mentor.

> I love it. It makes me reflect on my own practice and I often learn from the mentee. I love supporting new head teachers to get the best out of the school, the staff and the children. Every child deserves a good education. All I do is make the head reflect and have time to see things from different perspectives. I had one head who was having problems with lunchtimes. I took her to three different schools at lunchtime to see how they did it and she was able to use this to improve lunchtimes in her own school. I just asked her questions and showed other examples.

This is an example of how, when working right, mentoring has benefits for both mentee and mentor – something every mentor in the case studies throughout the book acknowledges. However, there are some serious things to consider before embarking on a mentoring process that can affect the outcomes.

- Mentoring is not a 'quick fix' and if you are an individual wanting mentoring it must regarded as a twelve-month commitment.

- An organizational scheme must have total commitment for two to three years to integrate mentoring as part of the culture.

- Mentoring is not a training programme and should not be promoted as such inside an organization.

- Don't make a mentoring scheme exclusive to only one group of employees. This sometimes happens in hierarchical organizations whereby mentoring is perceived for the top ranks only. All can benefit, ranging from new graduates to support staff. Otherwise mentoring becomes 'elitist'.

- Ensure the organization is ready for a long commitment to mentoring and has the vocal and active support of top management. In fact, the best way is to lead by example. Too often those at the top say they don't require development and this gives a negative message that learning and development is only for the 'lower ranks'.

- Effort has to be made on a regular basis to maintain a mentoring scheme. Do not set it up and then leave it to administer itself. When a crisis hits, the tendency is to focus on the bottom line, whereas mentoring can generate additional measures to ensure longevity.

- Mentors need to be included in the learning process at the beginning to enhance their capabilities as mentors and must not be excluded from this. If someone tells you they don't need to learn to enhance their mentoring skills, they won't make a good mentor.

- Finally, while e-mail and the telephone are useful, face-to-face mentoring sessions are best and should not be replaced if at all possible. If, for example, we have heavy snow making travel difficult, video conferencing or the telephone may be required but should be followed up with a face-to-face meeting soon after.

All these and other pitfalls will be addressed in the book but these points need to be made clear at the start. Language is important too. Here, the person who is meeting with the mentor will be referred to from this point on as the mentee.

Throughout the book the most common questions when setting up a mentoring scheme will be answered. Being a mentor is a wonderful gift and legacy to give to someone. Having the support and wisdom of a mentor is a dynamic process of moving forward. This manual will guide you on how to set up a sustainable mentoring scheme in your organization. At the end of each chapter there will be an opportunity to reflect on what has been read. Having explained why mentoring is needed today, it is now beneficial to explain exactly what is meant by mentoring.

What is mentoring?

To understand a concept in our language such as mentoring, it is always helpful to unravel its history for it shows how a concept formed and that language reflects how we see reality. The concept of mentoring didn't begin as a verb but with a person in an old story. *The Odyssey* by the Greek Homer tells the adventures of Odysseus on his way home after the siege of Troy around 1200 BC. Before going off to fight, Odysseus left a guardian for his household to help bring up his son, Telemachus. This guardian's name was Mentor. Over the 10 years that Odysseus was away Mentor acted as teacher, adviser, friend, guide and surrogate father to Telemachus.

It was customary in Ancient Greece for young male citizens to be paired with older males to ensure that young men learned the values of their mentor, who would often be a friend of the young man's father. The belief in Greek society was that young men would learn skills, knowledge, values and culture from others who could share this wisdom.

However, some may argue that Mentor did not carry out his duties satisfactorily as other kings gate-crashed and tried to force Penelope, wife of Odysseus, to marry one of them while trying to find ways to rid themselves of her son Telemachus. It was the intervention of the goddess Athena that helped keep Telemachus safe and enabled Odysseus to win his land back. Author Karen Klinke writes 'Like all good mentors, Athena imbued Telemachus with a sense of courage and morality and set him off on a journey to explore his leadership potential' (Roberts, 1999). Good mentors touch your life, not just your career, and often see in us more than we can see ourselves.

Andy Roberts wrote an article suggesting that 'Mentor... was simply an old friend of King Ulysses who largely failed his duties of keeping the King's household intact.' Roberts goes on to say it was 'the goddess Pallas Athena... who took Mentor's form so as to guide, counsel and enable both Odysseus and his son Telemachus through their journey' (Roberts, 1999: 81–90).

Roberts goes on to say that the view of Mentor as counsel, guide, teacher and adviser came not from Homer but the fifteenth-century French cleric and author Fenelon in *Les Aventures de Telemaque*, a continuation of the Odyssey story. It was here that Mentor is described as we understand today what a mentor should be.

Whatever the facts, mentoring is a concept we use in our everyday language that has developed over time. In the Middle Ages craft guilds took on young boys and they learned from a master who acted as a mentor. The young man lived in the master's house and was guided by him until the young man became a master himself. Through this process developed the merchants, goldsmiths and lawyers that became part of our structured society. Using this approach to mentoring, the next generation of skills developed. The craft guilds controlled and maintained the quality of work and the wages of their profession. It was later that the word mentor was added to the *Oxford English Dictionary*, as a noun, in 1750.

Between 1793 and 1796 *The Female Mentor* was published, and a copy can still be found in the British Library today. It is a collection of texts based on a woman called Amanda, who, as a mother, set up and led a discussion group for her children. The group discussions were so popular that many others wanted to join them and eventually through demand, the collection was published. The title came after one of Amanda's children said: 'Indeed, Madam, I will always follow your advice, for you are our Female Mentor.'

The Industrial Revolution changed the master–apprentice relationship to one of employer–employee, whereby the focus of the employer moved away from maintaining quality to increasing profits. Instead of developing skilled individuals, people were perceived as a resource like the machines they worked at. Low wages and long hours resulted in the development of trade unions and the turbulent era of management versus worker. Mentoring took on a machine-like quality and the mentor was described as 'pulling strings' or 'putting the wheels in motion'. People still within the Industrial Age paradigm use this language today and it needs to be challenged. Mentoring today is a sophisticated relationship between two people whereby experience and wisdom is used to enable a person to reflect, question and construct actions while being able to tap on doors that would otherwise be closed. The concept of mentoring has survived, grown and is not only viable today but needed.

A human need

It is a fact that as human beings we often actively seek out a mentor. We look to bond with someone who has the perceived wisdom to teach and guide us. Likewise, a mentor may see a youthful energy and enthusiasm in a mentee that triggers a desire to teach and nurture. There are those who suggest the mentor gains a physiological benefit through increased levels of oxytocin in the body and that there are social benefits for both mentee and mentor.

Others perceive mentoring as a form of learning. However, mentoring is more than a learning process to developing technical skills, understanding the organizational culture or identifying the next role in a person's career. In the case studies included throughout the book, you will begin to see that mentoring has many benefits.

David Clutterbuck, who has raised the profile of mentoring in the UK, describes the process as: 'Mentoring supports a process that is about enabling, supporting, sometimes triggering, major change in people's life and work. As such it is about developing the whole person, rather than training in particular skills' (Clutterbuck, 1991).

Mentoring or coaching?

Some organizations will state that they have a mentoring scheme where the line manager is supposedly mentoring a junior. This is more likely to be coaching – focusing on performance or just technical skills. With the rapid rise of coaching in the last few years, there is often confusion between mentoring and coaching – but there are key differences.

- A coach doesn't have to have the skills and experience of the person they are coaching. Their skill is to listen and ask questions to help the client resolve the issue.
- The focus of coaching is usually, though not always, developing performance in their present role.
- Mentoring develops potential, helping the mentee go beyond their present role.
- Mentoring isn't what a person does but a role to help another and it may include coaching.

There is also confusion sometimes over the difference between a role model and a mentor. Having role models is also beneficial to learning and development but there is no particular structure in a role modelling relationship. It is usually based on observation where the observer sees positive behaviour to emulate from a role model. For example, a team leader models how to work effectively and treat everyone with respect so that team members who go on to be team leaders can see how they can behave to be effective also. A previous team leader of the RAF Red Arrows explained to me how as a team member he learned from a good team leader who modelled how effective and trustworthy a team leader could be. He also shared with me how he learned from another team leader how not to lead. Good role models are important to learning and tend to exhibit:

- exceptional behaviour in how they achieve their goals and do things;
- success through integrity;
- enjoyment of their work and achievements;
- knowledge and understanding of the organization, its culture and policies;
- how to influence and improve things;
- influencing several people as a role model.

Mentoring, on the other hand, is more structured, on a one-to-one basis, whereby each has a clear expectation of the other. However, the mentor also has a function as a role model.

Mentoring is person-centred. This means:

- the mentee generates their goals;
- the mentor has a genuine desire to help people;
- the learning is transformational.

The litmus paper test for mentoring (Figure 1.1) is that there is real change at a cognitive, behavioural, learning and practice level.

FIGURE 1.1

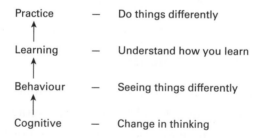

In other words, there should be a change in thinking, ways of seeing things; of understanding how to learn as well as doing things. This is described well by Julie Hay, who distinguishes learning as:

- Traditional learning is learning how to do things, by being taught or observing.

- Transitional learning is learning how to do things differently, ie improvement.

- Transformational learning is a complete change of perspective, altering the mentee's worldview and including an understanding of how to learn.

When mentoring is transformational and person-centred, it is as David Clutterbuck describes 'one of the most powerful developmental approaches available to individuals and organizations' (Clutterbuck, 1998).

If we return to the source of mentoring, it was the guidance of Athena and Odysseus at the end of *The Odyssey* that enabled Telemachus to become a wise warrior himself and help expel the invaders. Left alone, he would probably have been slain by one of the other kings. We can now define mentoring as Andy Roberts (2000) explains it:

A formulised process whereby a more knowledgeable and experienced person actuates a supportive role of overseeing and encouraging reflection and learning within a less experienced and knowledgeable person, so as to facilitate that person's career and personal development.

Is it worth having a mentor?

Organizations spend millions of pounds on learning and development but there is plenty of evidence that shows transferring that learning into a meaningful context at work is not often forthcoming. Were the Greeks right in using mentoring to develop people? The consulting firm Heidrich and Struggles surveyed 1,250 executives to establish what had enabled their success. Nearly two-thirds said they had had a mentor. The report added, 'Executives who had a mentor earned more money at a younger age, are happier with their progress, and derive greater pleasure from their work' (Roche, 1979).

A good mentoring scheme is such a rich source of learning that it can be used with young people in schools, graduates in their first work role, new employees, executives, diverse groups, older people who need to learn new skills from a younger person, and employees new to a country. The scope is vast. Organizations can incorporate mentoring to:

- prepare potential high-flyers for senior management;
- attract quality recruits;
- retain the best talent;
- improve equal opportunities;
- reinforce cultural change;
- demonstrate new ways of working;
- release potential across the whole organization.

So it is really important to understand the true meaning of mentoring and how it applies today.

The essence of mentoring and its benefits

According to the dictionary, the word 'essence' means 'most important feature of something that determines its identity'. What sets mentoring apart from coaching and other forms of learning is the ability to enter into real 'dialogue' with another person.

Dialogue is a multifaceted process that goes beyond conversation, discussion and coaching. Dialogue again comes from the Greeks, in particular Socrates, and is derived from the Greek word *dialogos*, which means word or meaning, passing through. The work has been developed more recently. The philosopher Martin Buber first used the term dialogue in 1914 to mean not just a discussion but rather as a way of people appreciating each other as human beings. However, it is the work of physicist David Bohm that has contributed most to the concept of dialogue and has now been taken up by William Isaacs at the Massachusetts Institute of Technology (MIT) in the United States. Bohm suggested dialogue as a form of conversation that should focus on bringing to the surface and altering the 'tacit infrastructure' of thought. When people talk they do not only share words but meaning too. Through dialogue individuals learn to suspend their defensive exchanges and ask why those exchanges exist. In this way, Isaacs defines dialogue as 'a sustained collective enquiry into the processes, assumption and certainties that compose everyday experience' (Isaacs, 2000).

Dialogue explores our closely held values, the patterns of our thought processes, our mental models, the intensity of our emotions, our memory, inherited cultural myths and beliefs, and the way we structure moment to moment experience. The process questions our deeply held assumptions, beliefs, culture, meaning and identity. In summary, it tests our definitions of work, organizations and life. Brockbank and McGill (1998) describe the dialogue appropriate for mentoring as that which 'engages the person at the edge of their knowledge, sense of self and the world'.

In dialogue with a mentor, the mentee is able to recognize his or her assumptions and views and develop a new understanding, replacing defensive behaviour and feelings of isolation. Through dialogue, learning that is transformational begins. It is where the mentee learns through the experience of the other person and can face their own feelings as they reflect. Reflective dialogue brings to the surface the mentee's realities and subjective experience, giving space for them to then consider what they need to do. The learning is experiential and comes from within rather than from the outside world as it would if you were listening to a trainer telling you what to do.

In addition, learning that is transformational occurs in behaviour through addressing fears, perceptions and assumptions about ourselves and others. Through dialogue with another, individuals gradually learn to suspend their defensive behaviour and probe into the underlying reasons for why they exist.

Therefore mentoring has this powerful ability for real transformation that goes far beyond improving performance or developing new skills. It is through intention, dialogue and reflection that mentoring is a really cost-effective way of developing people and organizations.

Having deeply understood what mentoring is we will now explore how this works and how to set up a mentoring scheme. Before that, take five minutes to reflect here and answer the questions below.

REFLECTIVE ACTIONS

- Mentoring is a concept and process that is as relevant today as in the past. What relevance does mentoring have for you?

- As human beings we actively seek out a mentor. Has anyone acted as a mentor to you in your life so far? What impact did it have?

- Mentoring not only involves sharing wisdom but also getting the mentee to think and behave in a way that requires a deep understanding of themselves and others. What effect would this have on the people in your organization?

Chapter Two
Mentoring
in organizations

Setting up a mentoring scheme is not a quick process and in a large organization should have a small team (a minimum of two) to follow the steps we are now going to take you through. This is to ensure that a mentoring scheme is right for the organization at the time it will be launched. It really is similar to launching a new 'product' or service and an organization would not do this unless they were sure the market was ready, the product was excellent and there was an effective way to establish and monitor its success. This chapter takes you through the pre-scheme stage – in other words, all the work that is required before the scheme is implemented.

Is your organization ready for a mentoring process?

To set up a mentoring scheme in your organization you need to be sure the organization is 'ready' and that people will participate. Do not rush each of these steps. The process begins with a list of questions, each of which should be answered in full. If you do not know any of the answers, then you will need to find them out. Do not set up a scheme without having this knowledge. Answering these questions will also tell you if you are the right person to drive the scheme forward.

- What are the driving forces for the organization?

- What are the key objectives for the next three years?

- Are people treated as a resource or as having the ability to add value, be innovative and take responsibility?

- What are the challenges facing your organization?

- What are the gaps between the challenges and the capabilities within it?

- Would a mentoring scheme resolve this?

- Will the culture actively support a mentoring scheme?

- What would your role be?

- Who else would be driving the scheme?

- Do you have the time to commit to this?

You may not be able to answer all the questions; therefore, this first step involves identifying and pulling together an advisory group/board to gather information and develop the policies and procedures for the scheme. An advisory team of senior people across functions and including board representation will give the scheme credibility and more likelihood of success.

The next set of questions to ask includes:

- Who is likely to leave over the next five years and what knowledge and experience will they take with them? How relevant is it to the organization?

- How is the current economic climate affecting the organization and what are the expectations and plans in place to deal with this? How will this affect the capabilities within the organization?

- Are enough people suitable to be promoted, take on additional responsibility and make decisions?

The second step is to work with a small group and develop scenarios. This is because facts alone are insufficient. Great scientists such as Einstein used imagination and storytelling to enable them to 'think outside the box'. Scenarios are stories about how the future might be for your organization in a way that helps recognize and adapt to changing aspects of the environment it operates in and the uncertainties that occur. From this process you will be able to see how mentoring could shape the future in your organization. A suggestion is to consider three scenarios: one based on doing nothing at all; the second on offering mentoring; the third on developing a world-class mentoring scheme for a sustainable future. However, never write more than three scenarios.

Step three is to scope the mentoring scheme. Does the need for developing people extend across all functions and all levels? Should it start with a target group who have to deal with a new initiative? This often is a good starting point and a smaller programme can be evaluated. While leading by example is important, try not to start with just the executive team.

Step four is to establish how ready the organization is to try and get a feel for how many people would put themselves forward to be either a mentor or mentee. Where are they in the organization? How many of the top team would put themselves forward? This question is very important. Are there enough mentors to mentees? Try not to match a line manager with a level below them. A mentoring scheme is far more effective if the two participants have a couple of levels between them. Also ask how cross-functional would it be for both mentors and mentees?

Step five is to consider some logistics such as:

- What if a mentor and mentee didn't 'hit it off'? What would be the procedure for ending the relationship without blame on either side?

- How would mentoring fit in with other initiatives and learning and development?

- What would threaten the mentoring scheme?

The sixth step is to establish how the mentoring scheme would be evaluated. This needs to be done before the scheme is set up and must include support from the executive. The best place to begin is where the organization is now with regard to data on recruitment, all learning and development, turnover of people and promoting within the organization.

Evaluation needs to establish two things:

1 how well the mentoring process is working within the organization;

2 how the process is adding value to the organization and its people.

In doing this, evaluation should enable the process to improve in quality and grow. Unlike most training courses a successful mentoring scheme must include line managers of the mentees in negotiating the agreement and assessing how it has worked. This early commitment is vital in changing a culture and mindset that believes learning and development is the responsibility of the human resources section.

Evaluation can include regular reports from mentors, mentees and line managers using interviews and analysing internal promotions. Hence the need for the data before the scheme begins.

The final step is to decide how you would communicate the scheme across the organization and even externally if you want mentors from outside the organization. It is important that all employees understand the scheme, and even what it is not. Rumours can abound, such as 'those on the scheme have been identified for promotion', resulting in 'them and us' behaviours that damages performance.

The information should include criteria for participating – remember how this will affect people. For example, will part-time people feel excluded? Information should also be clear about:

- the joining process and whether mentoring is carried out on company time;

- whether being on the scheme does, or does not, guarantee promotion;

- whether mentors are rewarded for their time;

- the process for ending a mentoring relationship that isn't working.

Organizations have various reasons to set up such a scheme, ranging from addressing a specific issue to resolving succession planning. People in the organizations will ask why time and effort is being used to set up a mentoring scheme and it is wise to have worked this out and keep asking in the planning stage: why are we doing this?

Therefore there is much work to be done before setting up a mentoring scheme but doing this will save time later and ensure success. The aim is to have a facilitated mentoring scheme that is simple, flexible and effective and that through positive mentoring relationships behaviour change and new learning for all parties can be evaluated at both the individual and organizational levels. At this stage, it is useful to have an idea of what success will look like.

Success factors involve:

- a process that supports the goals and needs of the organization;

- a way of selecting one or more priority groups as mentees;

- support from line managers and the top level of the organization;

- strategies for identifying the development needs of mentees;

- a way of identifying and qualifying mentors;

- an accessible way for matching mentors and mentees based on learning needs, compatibility and access;

- development of both mentees and mentors to prepare them for the responsibilities and skills they will require for positive, productive relationships;

- a code of practice and agreement that both parties can sign up to;

- a small team responsible for maintaining and supporting the different stages;

- an evaluation process to continuously improve the initiative;

- a final evaluation to assess the process that includes identifying outcomes for the individuals and the organization.

The box lists questions you need to ask before the scheme is set up.

Actions

Am I and the organization ready for a mentoring scheme?

What issues/needs do we have that would benefit from a mentoring scheme?

Do we have support, commitment and resources from the executive for this?

How will they demonstrate their commitment?

How are we going to set up the pilot mentoring system in relation to:

- A target group?
- Levels of the hierarchy?
- Cross-functions?
- Size of pilot?
- Duration of pilot?
- Duration of each mentoring relationship?

Are there enough mentors and at the right level in the organization?

Will we run this on a voluntary basis?

Will we encourage cross-functional mentoring relationships?

How will mentoring fit with other development activities?

Who will establish the policies and procedures?

Who will support and evaluate the scheme?

How will we evaluate the pilot?

How will we communicate the mentoring process across the organization?

How will we reward success?

If you are leading the project there is additional information you need to understand and that is how adults learn. It is important to understand how learning and mentoring work together.

How adults learn

Before setting up a mentoring scheme it is imperative to have an understanding of how adults learn to ensure the scheme fulfils its purpose. Therefore I'm going to broadly outline the main theories and show common characteristics to enable you to produce a model for learning that can be used for mentoring.

Learning tends to be a social process: that means it includes the context, conditions and culture. As such, how we understand the world is influenced by our life experiences and how we create meaning through the interactions with others using language. This is why mentoring is such a good process for learning and can be incorporated into any of the following 'models'.

Lewin developed an experiential model for learning which he described as a continuous circle whereby a person goes through the process of (1) having a concrete experience, (2) making observations and reflections on that experience, (3) forming abstract concepts and generalizations based on those reflections and then (4) testing those ideas in a new situation which leads to another concrete experience. Therefore learning here is based on a four-stage cycle.

In this model the person begins with a concrete experience, and fundamental to the process are feedback processes. Lewin actually borrowed the concept of feedback from electrical engineering to describe a problem-solving process at the heart of learning. Lewin believed that individual and organizational ineffectiveness was caused by both inadequate feedback processes and an imbalance between observation and action. What this means is that people at work either spend too much time data gathering and not enough on action or are consistently reacting and do not spend enough time getting the right information to begin with.

Mentoring would enable people to take a step back and have time to reflect. This would enable them to either consider what actions are needed and how to carry them out or stop reacting and instead take time to think and plan based on more information.

Dewey's model of learning is similar to Lewin's, although Dewey is more specific in the development nature of learning in that it transforms feelings and desires of concrete experience into higher purposeful action. He wrote:

> It involves: (1) observation of surrounding conditions;
> (2) knowledge of what has happened in similar situations in the past, a knowledge obtained partly by recollection and partly from the information, advice and warning of those who have had a wider experience; and, (3) judgment, which puts together what is observed and what is recalled to see what they signify. A purpose differs from an original impulse and desire through its translation into a plan and method of action based upon foresight of the consequences of action under given observed conditions.
>
> (Dewey, 1938: 69)

Here, stage two is where mentoring has a role to play in the learning process. However, the mentor's role isn't just based on experience. As Dewey says:

> Experience does not go on simply inside a person. It influences the formation of attitudes of desire and purpose. But this is not the whole of the story. Every genuine experience has an active side which changes in some degree the objective conditions under which experiences are had.
>
> (Dewey, 1938: 69)

In other words, learning through experience should change how we see things and act. A mentor assists in this process.

FIGURE 2.1   The way we learn: Kolb's learning cycle

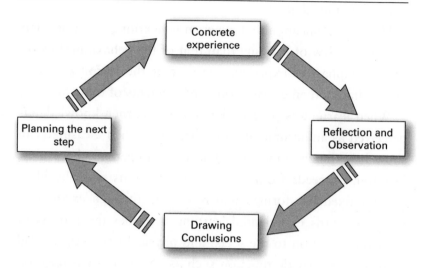

David Kolb (1948). *Experiential Learning. Experience as the source of Learning and Development,* Prentice-Hall

Kolb expanded this view of how learning from experience differed from, for example, our educational system, because ideas, rather than being fixed, are formed and re-formed through experience and is a process of human adaptation to the social and physical environment. In addition, Kolb regarded learning as more than a brain activity of cognition or perception. Rather, learning according to Kolb involved thinking, feeling, perceiving and behaving. In other words, learning involves our whole being. A good mentor would include how the mentee was feeling, thinking, perceiving and behaving as part of the learning process.

Piaget regarded learning as something that occurred between the individual interacting with the environment that is similar to the learning models of Lewin and Dewey. This interaction fell into two areas: accommodation (to experience in the world) and assimilation (of experience from the world). For Piaget, the key to learning lies in the mutual interaction of accommodation (adapting our mental concepts based on our experience in the world) and assimilation (integrating our experience into existing mental models).

What is significant about experiential learning is that it offers a different view of learning than that of the behavioural theorists. It emphasizes experience as part of the learning process rather than outcomes based on fixed elements of thought.

When learning is perceived as outcomes, then knowledge is perceived as an accumulation of facts that when measured can show how much someone has learned. Experiential learning, however, proceeds from different assumptions whereby ideas are not fixed but formed and re-formed through experience. In other words experiential learning describes the process of human adaptation to the social and physical environment and involves not a single function such as cognition or perception but the total person, including thinking, feeling, perceiving and behaving. Hence a good mentor will include all these functions as part of the learning process.

The more real the experience that is acquired, the more the mental model is enriched.

These mental models represent a person's view of the world as well as the context to view and interpret new information. Mentoring enables people to recognize their mental models and explains why new information is perceived the way it is, which will be different from someone with different experiences and mental models. So what are mental models?

Mental models and learning

Mental models represent the way we look at the world and are influenced by the age we live in, the context and our knowledge. An example is how our mental model of the world has changed since our understanding of bacteria became known. In 1857 Louis Pasteur was trying to resolve the problem of wine spoilage, as wine was one of the main beverages in France. He discovered what we call the biogenesis of life, ie life comes from life and that it is micro-organisms, or bacteria, that spread contagious diseases. Until then it was believed that such diseases were a curse or caused by bathing too frequently!

As our mental models of the world changed because of Pasteur's discovery, our behaviours also changed in how we prepared food, recognizing the importance of sanitation and particularly of washing hands and sterilizing equipment. Therefore, learning includes the transfer of knowledge between individuals and shared mental models. These mental models then determine how we take action. The problem is that they lie below our level of awareness. Mentoring can bring mental models to the surface and question the assumptions underlying them, enabling the mentee to gain a new perspective.

Senge describes mental models as deeply held internal images of how the world works, which have a powerful influence on what we do and the actions we take, because they also affect what we see. Senge says 'Because it's so hard to see mental models, you may need the help of another person, a ruthlessly compassionate partner. In the quest to uncover the reality of our own mental models, we are each other's greatest assets' (Senge, 1990). Having a trusting mentor to undertake this role is truly helpful in understanding why we are where we are and whether something is holding us back.

However, mental models also affect mentors. Moreton-Cooper and Palmer (2000) found disabling traits in mentors they describe as:

> first the rigid, stereotypical mind with set values and ideas, found in bureaucratic organizations, so a danger in the public service sector; second, the ego mind, self interested and self important, unable to share but typically entrepreneurial so a danger in business; and third, the Machiavellian mind, devious and calculating, obsessed by power and politicking, a danger anywhere.
>
> (Moreton-Cooper and Palmer, 2000)

Senge had earlier written:

> One thing all managers know is that many of the best ideas never
> get put into practice. Brilliant strategies fail to get translated
> into action. This 'slip 'twixt cup and lip' stems not from weak
> intentions, wavering will, or even non-systemic understanding,
> but from mental models. More specifically, new insights fail to get
> put into practice because they conflict with deeply held internal
> images of how our world works, images that limit us to familiar
> ways of thinking and acting.
>
> (Senge, 1990)

The phenomenon by which experiences create individual mental
models is often called 'double-loop learning'. It is rich, positive
mental models that organizations need to share between employees or through a mentoring process. Key to the mentoring
process is to understand that it is only when what is learned re-
enters the environment through action can we learn something
from someone else.

Argyris and Schon

The descriptions single- and double-loop learning were first
used by Argyris and Schon (1996) to distinguish learning for
improving how things are done. Learning here goes beyond
improving a situation to transforming the situation. Single-loop
learning can achieve improvement but doesn't question how we
see things. Double-loop learning is where assumptions, beliefs
and values that resulted in where we are are challenged and con-
sequently transformed and can literally change the way we see
the world. In other words, new understanding comes when the
tacit is made explicit and mentoring should question tacit
knowledge.

From these models it is clear that mentoring is a deep way of
learning that when done correctly, through dialogue and reflective practice, provides transformational learning, new insights,
perspectives and ways forward. Learning should involve a change

in behaviour that begins at the cognitive level. To make it easier for learning, it is useful to know your 'learning style'. During the 1980s human resources (HR) specialists, Honey and Mumford developed a process for people to discover their preferred way of learning. It explains why some learning is easier than others. Having this knowledge and understanding in a mentoring relationship will enable it to be more effective. The questionnaire and self-analysis is at the end of the book for your use.

One final note, and that is to do with the mindset of the mentor. Research has shown that people respond better to positive feedback and want their mentor to have a positive outlook in order to develop their full potential. An experiment was undertaken into how people improved as a result of feedback. One group was told only their strengths, the other, only their weaknesses. Those given feedback on what was positive improved at a faster rate. Outside of an experimental situation, most would want a balance. The key is to begin with the positive first and then follow with what needs improving.

The role of mentor is complex and can't be left to chance. Therefore identifying the right mentors and developing them is crucial. But it all begins by checking where the organization is so that the context is right.

REFLECTIVE ACTIONS

- Have you checked whether the organization is ready for a mentoring process?
- What did you find?
- What is your main objective for setting up the scheme?
- What did you discover from how adults learn?
- How can this understanding be incorporated into your mentoring scheme?

Chapter Three
Finding the right people

Identifying mentors

What are you looking for in a mentor? Mentors should not be chosen purely on position and experience. In fact it is important to judge mentors by their behaviours, qualities and how they provide support and enable others. You are looking for individuals who are both capable and committed to help another person develop. This part of setting up a mentoring scheme requires your utmost focus for it ensures the effectiveness of mentoring relationships.

Organizational life encourages self-interest and self-promotion. A mentor has had to work at breaking patterns such as 'knowing best', fixing problems, controlling, feeling important and needed. A mentor has to focus on the other person, not just by listening but by seeing things from the other person's perspective, being authentic and emotionally intelligent. Therefore, these are the key elements you need to assess possible mentors for.

Person-focused

A good mentor is so focused on the mentee that they push away thoughts and conversations in their head of what they want to say such as 'Ah yes, I had that experience and I will tell you how I handled it.' A mentor isn't required to problem solve or 'fix' things. They must listen actively and be in the present moment and put what they are hearing in the mentee's context, not their own. This is difficult and why mentors should always undergo development before acting as a mentor. A good mentor enjoys being with people and interacting with others – not as the centre of attention but genuinely listening to and learning about them.

Listen actively

This requires not only listening to the words of the other person but also the ability to pick up the non-verbal communication such as body language, facial expressions and tone of voice. Is the person angry or feeling lost?

The danger when listening is to be thinking 'I know how I'd deal with that problem', for this is identifying yourself in the other person and when you do this you miss what the mentee is feeling and dealing with in their environment. Instead a mentor needs to learn to put their solutions aside, not judge, and instead listen from the place where the mentee is and put yourself there. What is it about their problem in their context that is an issue? How a mentor follows up with questions is also important. There is a big difference between asking 'Why do you want the promotion?', which can sound critical or aggressive, and asking 'What is it that's attractive to you in this promotion?' The second question doesn't sound confrontational but is still searching.

From the non-verbal signals a mentor should also be able to see what is not being said or being distorted. So listening is actually quite complex and requires learning and development in itself before mentoring someone.

Knowledge of the organization

A mentor who knows the organization, its purpose, goals, vision, culture and values is really important in most cases.

Able to deal with emotions

Emotions can come from either mentor or mentee. How should a mentor deal with an emotional mentee? How does a mentor deal with their own emotions that are being triggered through the relationship – perhaps impatience or even anger? A mentor has to learn how to deal with these. Are tears genuine pain or manipulation? Does a mentor express their anger or own it and say how they feel?

Feedback

Only feedback that is useful, encouraging and constructive will help mentees. How do you know if you are setting up a scheme where the mentors will provide this?

Conclusion

No mentoring system can just make individuals mentors without the development they need for the role. It is imperative to include development for mentors no matter how experienced they may be. If a mentor refuses this, then that tells you they do not have the right character to be a good mentor.

Finding the mentors

Finding your mentors will require two questions and two approaches. The questions to ask are:

- Where will the mentors come from?
- Will they be willing to give the time, energy and commitment?

Organizations' schemes can include internal mentors, external mentors or a mix of both. You have to decide what resources you have and which is the best way to establish your pool of mentors. The two approaches are to either ask for volunteers or to ask for nominations or recommendations. If you ask for volunteers it is best to state upfront that not all volunteers will be selected but that all will attend a short programme to develop mentoring skills and behaviours. If you ask for recommendations or nominations, then ask why they are being put forward with an example.

In both approaches you are seeking people who can demonstrate:

- willingness to help people grow and develop;
- leadership;
- credibility with their peers and those they will be mentoring;
- they are people-centred;
- strong interpersonal skills, especially empathy;
- they can take responsibility;
- they are good communicators;
- they know how to use personal power and influence to get things done;
- they can be a positive role model;
- willingness to use development plans and give honest feedback;
- knowledge about the organization, its environment and goals;
- belief in team spirit and have a willingness to share information and knowledge.

Also, for both approaches, make it easy for people to respond and be clear about the information you need. This should include:

- name and present role;
- education;
- summary of experience;
- why they wish to be a mentor;
- time they can give;
- constraints, for example travel-time commitments.

The next stage is to put possible mentors through a screening process, followed by more detailed interviews, and moving on to their development programme. Remember that mentors need to feel valued and motivated to provide the time required. How will you enable them to feel valued and how can you reward them? One way is to include the mentoring role in the annual appraisal. Another is to provide a certain amount of time off, or being featured in the internal newsletter, giving the scheme a high-profile name or perhaps an opportunity for further educational study. Different rewards will suit different mentors, so some flexibility is required.

Benefits from mentoring

It's important mentors experience benefits from the time they commit as a mentor. These include:

- Fresh motivation in work: Mentors often remark that through mentoring someone it enhances their motivation and enables them to take a fresh look at their own role and how they achieve things.

- A personal interest in another person: Having focused on their own career, mentors sometimes develop a personal interest in the career of someone else and want them to succeed.

- New learning and development: Mentors have told me that they learn as much from a mentoring relationship as the mentee. It seems that by questioning the mentee they end up also questioning their own behaviour and realize they could be an even better role model if they learned from the sessions also.

- Keeping abreast of the environment: Through mentoring someone mentors become more aware of the context and environment in which they operate and sometimes see things with fresh eyes that enables them to also see things from a different perspective.

Dangers from mentoring

You need to be aware of a number of possible dangers:

- Lacking the right skills: No one should go into mentoring without development first. If the mentor lacks skills the relationship will suffer and the mentor's reputation could be tarnished.

- Time pressure: Taking on any mentoring role is a long-term commitment and there will be times when work pressure may require a mentor to cancel sessions. This may happen once in twelve months but it shouldn't happen more than that. It is important that the mentor regards this work as an important part of their role and not an 'extra'.

- Being controlling: If a mentor is controlling they won't allow the mentee to find their own route through organizational politics and work. This undermines the mentee and their confidence will diminish. Even worse, the mentor may take on some of the mentee's tasks to ensure success that will be a good reflection on being mentored by that individual.

What a mentee is looking for is a mentor who can:

- establish and build a rapport;
- listen actively;

- have a positive mental attitude;
- ask insightful questions;
- provide feedback;
- signpost sources of help;
- have the commitment to achieve agreed goals and actions.

For these reasons it is vital to spend time ensuring the right people become mentors, have the right development and are supported. How you keep track of mentors is also important and goes beyond maintaining a simple database. Capturing the impact of the scheme, the outcomes from individuals who have had a mentor and bottom-line improvement are required over a long time.

There is so much to consider at this stage it is useful now to reflect.

REFLECTIVE ACTIONS

When creating a mentoring pool you need to answer the following:

- How will we recruit mentors?
- What are the skills, characteristics, experiences we want the mentors to have?
- How will we recognize and reward mentors?
- What and how will we communicate to attract mentors?
- How can we make it easy for people to volunteer or respond to come forward?
- How are we going to assess volunteer mentors?
- What system do we need to record and maintain the list of mentors?
- What do we include in the description of the mentor's role?

- What should we include in the day's induction and development of mentors?
- How can we ensure that mentors share the credit with their mentees?

Finding the right mentees

What is your aim in setting up a mentoring scheme? Who is the target group and why?

There are many reasons for setting up a mentoring scheme but the main reasons are usually either to resolve a problem with succession planning and to develop the next top executives, or to ensure you retain and develop the best talent. However, be careful that a mentoring scheme does not become an elite group disengaged from and resented by others.

Is there a target group? One of the reasons an organization sets up a mentoring scheme is that many people at the executive level are due to retire in the near future and so the strategy is to target second-line managers who have the capability to progress and take their place. Another common reason is an organization that offers a graduate scheme that includes mentoring.

When identifying mentees the key ingredient is to find people who will take responsibility for their growth and development. Work demands will always make learning and development a challenge so it is imperative that the motivation to fulfil their mentoring commitments is part of the person's character.

Most organizations use a self-nomination and line manager's nomination process but be aware that self-nomination can also be ego driven and the best individuals may be quieter and not always so confident. If you go down the self-nomination route it is important to clearly communicate the criteria for participation, what responsibility will lie with mentees and the expected outcomes. The first question to ask candidates is: 'Why do you want to do this?' If the desire is promotion it must be made clear at the outset that being part of a mentoring scheme is not a guarantee for promotion and that they and their mentor will be evaluated. It should also be made clear that there is no financial incentive to participate in the scheme. All this clarification is to ensure the right people participate.

Not all candidates may be accepted and you will have to deal with that while ensuring the motivation of those not accepted is not damaged. If you want to target specific skilled people or target groups the criteria should add 'In particular, we would like to receive nominations from...'. Groups who tend not to nominate themselves are office employees or secretaries who are also usually overlooked for learning and development. Yet remember the first impression an organization projects is usually through a receptionist or secretary.

You can ask line managers to nominate someone they believe would benefit from the scheme but make clear the criteria first. However, it is worth being aware that sometimes a line manager can feel threatened by a subordinate participating in a mentoring scheme and may not put forward good candidates. You need to be aware of any 'old boy's network', discrimination against women or underrepresented groups, nepotism or favouritism. Peers are usually far better at identifying someone suitable.

To summarize, you can use any of the following or all three.

- Anyone who wishes to participate may nominate themselves.

- Managers may nominate subordinates who they believe have the potential to develop.

- Candidates may be nominated by anyone who has had experience with assessing the potential of the candidate.

What are you seeking in a mentee?

You should expect to find people who:

- are willing and able to take responsibility for their own development rather than expect or wait for the organization to provide development;
- have a high level of motivation to set goals and implement strategies to achieve them;
- receive feedback positively and are open-minded to different perspectives, willing to share information and feelings as well as discuss issues honestly within the ethos of confidentiality and respect;
- are willing to take risks, try new ways of doing things and look for solutions to problems;
- seek challenging assignments and are willing to act on their initiative;
- are motivated by learning rather than just promotion and status;
- are reflective, making time and space to review their experience, values and skills and identify development needs;
- are willing to keep a learning log and personal development plan (PDP);
- are self-disciplined, following through on action plans and assignments;
- are enthusiastic and positive, prepared to exert effort, looking for opportunities and not passive in challenging situations.

Before they begin their work helping mentees, mentors will need to acquire skills in:

- identifying their own development needs and setting goals;
- developing and implementing an action plan;

- maintaining documentation on the learning and outcomes;
- keeping in regular contact with the coordinating team about progress and any problems.

Before the mentoring scheme begins, the organization and mentee must agree how the time for mentoring will be allocated. This may be entirely during working hours, during the mentee's own time or a mixture of both. In most situations, the time is during working hours, which demonstrates that learning and development is an important part of the job.

Establishing the mentee's development needs

Identifying development and learning needs can be achieved formally and informally. There are a multitude of assessment tools but my experience is that most people know the areas of themselves that require developing. In addition, the mentor will also have some knowledge of the key skills required as a person progresses in the organization.

The most important item the mentee needs is a personal development plan (PDP). It begins with establishing where the mentee is at that moment and their current reality. Also at the beginning the mentee has to decide how much time they will commit to mentoring. This reality check avoids disappointments later on. The development plan should be for at least 12 months and ideally cover 18 months, and should include:

- their favoured learning style;
- their objectives for mentoring;
- their strengths and weaknesses;
- what actions they will undertake;
- a review;
- what changes they have made.

On separate sheets within the PDP there should be a record of each goal, which is completed by the mentee. This should be set out as:

- the goal they wish to achieve in terms of outcome or result;
- the date by which they expect to accomplish the goal;
- the development skill or experience they wish to gain in measurable terms;
- the action steps they need to take;
- target dates for each step;
- what resources they require, such as information;
- a status report of where they have got to, for discussion with their mentor;
- the date of the discussion and what additional actions have been agreed.

A sample of what this could look like is below.

Personal development plan

Name: _____

Date: _____

Career goal: _____

Development objective: _____

Action Steps   Dates   Resources   Status and progress

REFLECTIVE ACTION FOR SOURCING MENTEES

- How will mentees be identified?
- How will we select them?
- How much time each month should be given to mentoring work?
- How do we encourage mentees to take responsibility for their own learning?
- What learning do they require before they begin?
- How will development needs be identified?
- What will the standard development plan look like?
- How often shall the development plan be reviewed and by who?
- What information do mentees need?

Chapter Four
The nuts and bolts of a mentoring scheme

Research has found that one mentoring scheme in three lasts less than two years and that two in three require revitalizing and improving. Therefore, if you are wondering why I am suggesting you spend so much time on planning, it is because time for planned nurturing of the scheme builds sustained relationships and raises the success factor. This in turn provides credibility and the spiral is upwards not downwards. Before you begin setting up a mentoring scheme there are two areas that must be confirmed.

1 you are really clear why you are setting up the scheme and its purpose;

2 you have support from the top of the organization that is more than verbal agreement. People have to model this by either being a mentor or using a mentor, including the executive team/board.

To achieve these two crucial areas you will have:

- carried out research to demonstrate the need;
- clarified what objectives would be achieved;
- decided how you would evaluate and show added value and even bottom-line goals;
- had constructive conversations with the top and feel confident about how the scheme will work.

The key is to balance the level of bureaucratic control and the need to help people have positive, sustainable mentoring relationships.

How the scheme will work

In deciding the structure you want to follow it is best to decide what is right for your own organization. Here are some models you can choose from. In the UK David Clutterbuck is regarded as a leader in the field of mentoring. His structure follows stages along the guidance of how intense the learning is during the mentoring relationship:

- beginning with rapport building, when the learning is small;
- to direction setting;
- followed by progress, when the intensity of learning is at its peak;
- then a decline as the relationship goes through maturation;
- and, finally, closes.

However, if you have not set up a mentoring scheme previously, a more detailed structure, process and application with the correct forms is required.

Administering the scheme

Large mentoring schemes require good administration. You will need to be ready to respond to questions such as 'My mentor is leaving the organization, who else do you have?' Good project management and a few effective systems are required.

This need not be complicated, for example a database with names, location and pairing can be put onto a spreadsheet, while mentors' biographies can be kept on file. The key is to maintain the database and keep it up to date.

Mentors need support, especially in knowing where to go for advice on challenging issues they are not equipped to deal with. For example, how do they deal with a situation where the mentee ends up with a serious 'crush' on the mentor – we are all human and these things do happen in organizations and need to be addressed rather than not talked about.

The best schemes bring mentors together every six months to share experiences or learn how to improve their mentoring skills further. These sessions not only give them support, but if run well are very motivating and rich with learning. After mentors have nominated themselves, it is the most effective time to provide them with development. No one should become a mentor without development – regardless of their role in the organization. This should cover an in-depth understanding of the roles of mentors and how to be effective.

At the same time, mentees need to have development at different stages. The first can introduce the concept of mentoring, including what to expect from their mentor, and can make it clear that they must take responsibility for driving the relationship. Again, after six months, mentees need to review their progress, and relate it to their personal development plan and the role of mentoring in their future career. Some organizations produce a handbook to support this.

When a mentor and mentee meet they need to be clear about the ground rules and the expectations both have for the relationship. This ensures no disappointments later. It also clarifies how the process will begin and continue, enabling both to then focus on the mentoring. I would suggest ground rules are typed up on a single sheet of paper as a simple list and discussed between the two parties at the start. For example:

- How often will you meet?
- Who will contact whom?
- How long will the sessions be?

- Who will keep time?
- What are the ground rules for cancellations?
- How will you both decide how much information is disclosed?
- What about confidentiality, and under what circumstances would someone else be involved?
- How will the mentee take responsibility for their own learning from the process?
- What are the expectations of both?
- Is there a right to stop if the process isn't working?
- Is there a timescale on how long the mentoring will last?
- How often will both reflect on how effective the process is?

Julie Hay sets this out as:

Procedural

Where?

When?

How frequently?

How long?

Professional

What specific aspect are we going to work on?

What does the learner want to achieve?

How does that sound to the mentor?

How are we going to work together?

Personal

How are we going to celebrate success?

How will we deal with setbacks or disappointments?

Psychological

How open, effective and trusting is the relationship between us?

Are there any particular or special issues we need to deal with?

Boundaries of the mentoring relationship should be agreed at the outset:

- between the mentor and mentee;
- with the mentee's line manager;
- within the aims and objectives of the organization.

When both parties are happy with the ground rules it is worth working through a code of conduct that will last for the duration of the meetings. The European Mentoring and Coaching Council (EMCC) have produced a standard for the industry.

EMCC code of conduct

1 Mentoring is a confidential activity, in which both parties have a duty of care towards each other.

2 Both mentor and mentee should be volunteers; either may dissolve the relationship if they feel it is not working.

3 The mentor's role is to respond to the mentee's developmental needs and agenda; it is not to impose his or her own agenda.

4 Mentor and mentee should respect each other's time and other responsibilities, ensuring they do not impose beyond what is reasonable.

5 Mentor and mentee should also respect the position of third parties, other members and colleagues.

6 The mentor should not intrude into areas that the mentee wishes to keep off-limits, unless invited to do so. Mentors should check this out with mentees and, where appropriate, suggest that mentees seek counselling.

7 Mentor and mentee should be open and truthful to each other about the relationship itself, reviewing from time to time how it might be effective.

8 Mentor and mentee share responsibility for the smooth winding down and proper ending of their relationship when it has achieved its purpose, or renegotiating a future relationship.

The quality and professionalism of the relationship is the major factor in ensuring an effective learning process. For this reason expectations must be realistic, including a 'non-romantic' view that a mentor will fix things.

When all this has been discussed and agreed an agreement can be signed by both parties if required. Those who use internal mentors often don't include this but it is essential for those using external mentors. An example of a mentoring agreement is included on page 65.

Direction and objectives

The next stage is to clarify the objectives for both parties. The danger here is for the mentee to rush to find an immediate solution to an immanent problem. It is far better to work through the direction both wish to go and the objectives so the decision of what issue(s) to tackle is more strategic. In addition, it gives both parties a structure for review and evaluation later.

Some people use SMART objectives:

Specific

Measurable

Achievable

Realistic

Time-bound

Another approach is based on Egan's seven-point goal-setting process. Here it states that:

1 Objectives should be stated using the 'past participle'. For example 'I want to stop smoking' becomes 'Within three months I will have stopped smoking completely.' Therefore the goals are achieved or acquired.

2 Objectives should be clear and specific, for example 'I want to be a better manager' isn't specific and needs to express what a 'better' manager means. For example, 'I will have improved my decision making and delegation skills by the end of next month.'

3 Objectives should be measurable and verifiable using clear statements such as 'My sales will increase by...'

4 Check that the necessary resources are available for the goal to be realistic.

5 The goal should be stretching as well as achievable.

6 The goal should be in congruence with the mentee's values to be achievable. Therefore, identification of values is part of the process.

7 A definite timescale is imperative – for example, 'I will complete the project by the end of November 2011.'

It is suggested that priorities are also identified and listed in order. This all keeps the process realistic and more likely to succeed.

A learning process through reflection

The meetings between mentor and mentee do not just involve talking. For learning to happen, reflection has to be included in the process. Reflection is best described by Alvesson and Willmott:

> A critical process that seeks to encourage the questioning of take-for-granted assumptions so to reflect critically on how the reality of the social world, including the construction of the self, is socially produced and therefore open to transformation.
>
> (Alvesson and Willmott, 1992)

David Clutterbuck (1998) describes this part of the mentoring process as 'Focusing their thinking down on one issue for a period of quality time... An inner dialogue takes place... allows the learner to reframe a problem in a way that makes it easier, or at least clearer, to deal with.'

We live in the West in a world where action is valued most and the result is that we often end up doing things twice or even three times rather than think things through before deciding on the correct action.

Reflective learning

Reflection is a personal cognitive process. When an individual reflects they take an experience from the world and internalize it in their mind, making connections to other experiences and filtering it through their own personal biases. If this process results in learning, and it doesn't always, the individual then develops a way to respond to the world that is different from that prior to the reflection. Therefore it can be said that reflection is the process of stepping back from an experience to ponder its meaning to the self through the development of inferences. Learning becomes the creation of meaning from past or current events that serves as a guide for future behaviour.

From our reflections we construct future action as part of the learning process. Through reflecting we should gain a new way of understanding an experience and through this we can decide different actions and new behaviours:

> While reflection is itself an experience it is not, of course, an end in itself. It has the objective of making us ready for new experience... A new way of doing something, the clarification of an issue, the development of a skill or the resolution of a problem.
>
> (Bpoud *et al*, 1985)

This reflective learning in the mentoring process enables mentees:

- to study their own decision-making process;
- to be constructively critical of their relationship with colleagues;
- to face problems and painful episodes;
- to analyse hesitations, skill and knowledge gaps;
- to identify learning needs.

Judy Sorum Brown (2006) describes it as 'time to see into their own processes, to disclose their feelings and thinking, their reservations and struggles'. Peter Senge explains his first experience of reflective practice under Chris Argyris. Senge and his colleagues were asked to recall a conflict situation with either a client or family member. They had to remember not only what was said but also what they were thinking and did not say. As Argyris worked with them it became clear that Senge and his colleagues had actually contributed to the conflict through their thinking and the generalizations they made about the other person and that this thinking determined what they said, their body language and how they behaved. Yet the generalizations were never communicated.

When reflection is used with dialogue the mentor draws out those generalizations. Therefore, it is vital that both mentor and mentee understand reflective practice as part of their development before taking on either role.

Another part of the learning process is to return to the goals set out in the beginning and for the mentee to repeat them. Do they still apply? How far have they been explored? What have you agreed to achieve them? A good tip to pass on to mentors is not to rely on just one strategy to achieve the mentee's goals. If the single strategy doesn't work you are left with unfulfilled goals. Therefore, through reflection, both can consider different means to achieving the goals. This increases the chances of success.

The focus is to ensure that the mentee has a learning experience that results in either improving how they do things at the least or to transform into the best they can be. At the end of each mentoring session it is important to review and agree what the mentee has learned and what actions they are going to take.

Using a learning journal

The best way to aid reflective learning is for the mentee to keep a learning journal. It charts the development of an individual's learning. The most common question asked is: What do I write in it? It should be used to capture the whole learning experience, including thoughts and feelings. If a mentee regards the mentoring process as a journey, then the journal is a private record of where they have been and hope to go.

It's a good idea to find a notebook with a cover that has meaning – whether it's the colour or the picture. The mentee can write or draw in it. Inside the mentee can record things that happen in work as well as the mentoring sessions. It should record the mentee's reactions, changes in beliefs and practice, and the effect of other people such as role models, networks or the mentor.

The journal can be used as often as the mentee wishes. Every couple of months it's a good idea to read what you have put in it and ask:

- What have I discovered about myself?
- What do I know now that I didn't before?

- What do I now understand about how I learn?
- How will all this information influence work in the future?
- How do I feel about this?

There are techniques a mentee can practice to aid their journal writing. These are exercises to help people develop the skills to keep a journal of their mentoring journey:

Exercise 1

List six events in your life that enabled you to move forward and develop. Then take one the events and write it out including how you felt at the time. This should take five minutes.

Exercise 2

Take five minutes to answer these questions:

- Who am I?
- What is my purpose in life?
- What do I want to achieve?

Then take time to read what you have written. What surprises you? How does what you have written make you feel?

Exercise 3

Take fifteen minutes to write under the heading 'Two years from today'. Think of all the things you will have done, people you will have seen, places and how you would feel.

As human beings we spend so much of our time doing things that we forget the skills of thinking, reflecting and writing. When a mentee looks back on what they have written while they have been part of the mentoring process, they will see in black and white the learning journey they have taken.

At the end of each mentoring session it should be agreed what actions are going to be taken, when and the planned outcomes. Then the meeting can be evaluated. Did both parties benefit from the meeting? Do they need to make any changes to improve their sessions and in between them?

Close

There is always a time to end the relationship and often both parties knows when this is. However, when learning stops it is a good idea to ask each other is it time to close the sessions and part. There is nothing wrong with a mentoring relationship that has expired. Everything has a time.

The third person in the mentoring relationship

In the process of a mentoring relationship there is also someone else to consider as well as the mentee and mentor – the line manager/boss.

It is not recommended that a person is mentored by their immediate line manager, though they do have a role in the process. A line manager who supports or even suggests mentoring for their team can be included in the meetings at different stages, perhaps at the three month or six month session. This is vital if the line manager feels threatened, resentful or suspicious of one of their people having a mentor who is higher in the hierarchy. The fear is that the mentee will pass over them in the promotion stakes as well as have access to information and contacts the line manager doesn't have. Therefore when setting up a mentoring scheme there needs to be agreement for dealing with this.

One way is to ask the line manager every now and then to give feedback to both the mentor and mentee of any progress or improvements they have noticed in the mentee. It enables the line manager to feel part of the development process and show an interest in the outcome.

In one example, at a bank, the mentor was expected to call the line manager and introduce themselves and make occasional calls to keep the line manager informed of what they were doing with the mentee. However, confidentiality was maintained between the mentor and mentee by no disclosure of personal issues.

My preference is to structure the process whereby the three meet up once a quarter for a short feedback session. It will also be an opportunity for the line manager to learn from the mentor. One of the key ways we learn is from observing a positive model of how to behave and do things. It also means three people have the opportunity to develop.

The relationship is also strengthened when the mentee takes full responsibility for setting their own development plan and implementing it in their day-to-day work. This enables the line manager to see the benefits of the mentoring relationship. To ensure the line manager is involved it is important to include the answers to these questions in your mentoring scheme:

- What input does the line manager have in the mentee's development plan?

- How are you going to gain commitment from the line manager from the start and continue through the mentoring process?

- How will the line manager become involved with the mentor?

- How will you encourage the line manager to learn from the mentor?

- How will the mentee integrate their development activities into their day-to-day work?

The matching process

This stage is really important in setting up a mentoring scheme and as such should have senior people, not necessarily HR, in the team. This is definitely not a role for a junior administrative person. So who is going to be in the team to set this up, implement it, monitor and evaluate the scheme? It is usually spearheaded by a senior person to enable the scheme to have credibility and access to the right people.

What is your strategic reason for setting up a mentoring scheme? This will dictate who you open up the scheme to. You should also have a copy of or knowledge of the business plan for the organization. If you are a public sector organization then you should have access to the strategy for promotion projections and the budget for implementing this scheme. In addition, you need to have the support of the top executives and their commitment to lead by example, by either developing to become a mentor or taking a mentor for themselves.

To communicate the scheme many organizations use their intranet or in-house publication. It is important that everyone involved knows who is in the team and how to contact them. A strong communication plan is needed and should include the impact and evaluation of the scheme. It's really important that the scheme maintains a high profile. The team must be prepared to deal with any problems that occur.

The bare minimum the team should do is:

- identify the goals for the scheme;
- identify the target mentees;
- set up a half day with the mentees to clarify the process and set realistic expectations;
- identify mentors;
- set up a day's development for mentors;

- oversee the matching of mentor to mentee;
- ensure both parties have the documentation they need, including learning logs, and sign any agreements;
- monitor the mentoring relationships at different stages;
- evaluate the outcomes.

Getting a clear agreement

Things can go wrong for a multitude of reasons. They range from the unrealistic expectations of the mentee to a line manager feeling threatened. Therefore it is wise to set things out in an agreement. In particular the agreement should stipulate the role of the mentor and the goals of the mentee.

Role of the mentor

In some mentoring schemes the role of the mentor is very clear, while in others it is very loose. This can range from: a clear process for sharing wisdom and experience; to the mentor just acting as a role model and having the mentee observe how they deal with situations or activities. Another example of the two types is where the mentor's role is to prepare the mentee for a specific new responsibility or to observe the mentee and give feedback. Therefore because of the different choices it is important that when setting up the scheme the role of the mentor is made clear and returns back to the question at the beginning: why are you setting up the scheme?

Goals of the mentee

The mentee should bring a draft of their development plan to the first meeting with the mentor and the person overseeing the scheme. The draft may have been developed with the support of the line manager or drafted by the mentee in the introductory learning session. A good mentoring development plan will include not only skills but also activities such as learning different cultural values, 'opening doors' to the network above them. However, it should be made clear that while mentoring can help the individual there is no guarantee that access to the network will be accepted.

An example of the worksheet for the introduction is below.

Example of worksheet for development planning

Expectations	What mentee can do	What mentor can do
Share new ideas	Ask for input	Act as sounding board
Improve personal style	Be open to feedback	Give honest feedback

The mentoring agreement will also contain other issues that are binding.

Confidentiality

The relationship between the mentor and mentee has to based on trust and confidentiality. This takes time but both must at least feel comfortable from the beginning as they share information. Therefore confidentiality parameters need to be agreed. The usual rule is that all things remain confidential except where drugs, alcohol, fraud or serious damage to the organization are involved. Therefore it is worth discussing how sensitive issues will be dealt with at the onset.

Frequency of meeting

This tends to depend on the development agreement. It is usually a monthly meeting lasting between two hours and half a day.

This is normally face-to-face but there may be an occasion when that becomes difficult. Then a telephone call or email may suffice. However, it is strongly recommended that alternatives to face-to-face meetings are only used in an emergency. If a mentor can't be available at a time when the mentee requires guidance, they will be very disappointed and it could break down the trust. At the same time, a mentee understands that a good mentor will be busy and will accept the odd change. The key is for both to try to commit to the mentoring relationship and this means attending the agreed meetings.

Duration

It is a good idea to agree at the beginning the approximate duration of the mentoring relationship. The advantage of this is that it instils a sense of urgency to ensure the development process happens while at the same time making it clear that the arrangement is temporary. One of the dangers of mentoring is that if it continues too long, the mentee can become dependent and that is unhealthy for both parties. It is also important to make it clear here that there is no guarantee of promotion at the end of the duration.

Terminating the agreement

In some instances the mentoring relationship doesn't work and it is better to terminate it than carry on and risk things becoming worse. At different stages it is always worth both parties asking the question 'Are we adding any value to our meetings?' If the answer is 'no' then the agreement needs a way of being terminated without fault, blame or unpleasantness. Then both can walk away without damage.

Pitfalls

Mentoring relationships sometimes fail, and often the reason is that the boundaries and procedures are not thought through and the relationship suffers. The reasons are:

- contextual – the organization is not sufficiently supportive or clear about why mentoring is important and its purpose;

- interpersonal – adverse reactions from third parties, or breakdown of trust between mentor and mentee;

- procedural – being over- or under-managed.

Another reason is that a mentoring partnership doesn't fit in with the underlying reason for the scheme. A real example is where the scheme was set up in an organization where promotion is important and so whether coaching or mentoring, the emphasis ended up being about enabling people to be promoted. Someone outside the promotion arena asked for a mentor to help her find a better way of prioritizing her work to cope with a large workload. She was given a mentor who wasn't a good match and after one meeting never heard from him again. She chased the mentor but eventually gave up. She is now looking for a mentor outside the organization. However, in most cases, mentoring is very effective, providing it is set up properly, and that is why all the practical help here is important. Getting agreement early on in an 'adult' way can be achieved using the following example.

Example of an agreement

Mentoring agreement

We are voluntarily agreeing to enter into a mentoring relationship with the aim and expectation that both parties will benefit as well as the organization. To ensure things run as smoothly as possible we will together clarify the basis of this relationship.

Confidentiality

Duration of the relationship

Frequency of meetings

Place and first three in the diary for

Specific role of the mentor

Objectives of mentee

We agree to a no-fault conclusion if one or both of us requires the mentoring relationship to end.

Mentor _____

Mentee _____

Date _____

The importance of putting a well-planned, formal process in place can be seen in the following case study.

CASE STUDY   Mentoring in the police service

Before 2004 informal mentoring was taking place at Gloucestershire Constabulary but it lacked support and recognition and it wasn't followed up. So it was decided that a structured approach should be taken. The mentors were retrained and the numbers were increased. Mentors now have a role profile with responsibilities and the scheme provides a certificate in professional development (CPD) for mentors.

The Learning and Development team oversee the new scheme and if a police officer or staff member requests a mentor for a specific reason, the coordinator sends them three mentor profiles from which they can choose but within a limit of no more than two ranks above them. From the three mentors offered the mentee states their order of preference. The mentor of first choice is then sent an email stating that the named person has requested them as a mentor and decides whether to agree or not. The challenge for mentors is not to take on too many mentees, so the first preference may not be possible.

Once agreed, the two people, with support from the coordinator, set out how the relationship will work, including the option to withdraw at any time. One of the mentors, Sarah, has been with the constabulary for over five years. She has been a mentor for four years and has worked with three people from different parts of the organization. She said 'The mentor training was really useful because it harnesses the skills you already use to a higher level, including listening, and questioning. The reality comes when you put it into practice with a mentee.'

The length of time a mentoring relationship lasts is around six to nine months and is usually to deal with a specific issue such as being better prepared for promotion or lacking confidence in a new role.

It is obvious that mentees are likely to benefit but what about the mentor? Sarah was quite clear about this.

I have found real personal benefits through mentoring that include developing greater understanding of my own skills to support others, understanding what motivates people and developing my own skills of questioning and problem solving. I have definitely gained as much myself as helping others because it's structured, whereas you don't always have the time to do this with your own staff. It's helped me understand how people operate and how to adopt your own style to work better. I would certainly recommend mentoring to others. You think it's going to be time-consuming, but, in reality, you get so much out of it as well as the satisfaction of being a helpful catalyst for others.

Daniel is a sergeant who joined the service at 18. Ten years later he realized that to progress he had to take responsibility for his own career. He had been aware of the mentoring scheme but it wasn't until he joined the High Potential Development Scheme that he decided part of his development required a mentor. So what was the appeal of mentoring? Daniel said:

Mentoring is a more formal process of spending time with a senior ranked officer. I chose someone I had known throughout my career and he has been a fantastic mentor. We've helped each other in some ways. But where he has really helped me is in enabling me to visit other forces and sections around the country and see the best of the best. It means I know where I want to go with my career.

Daniel is aiming to go to Warwick University to gain a Master's Degree and he describes this as 'the best opportunity I'll ever have!' What does he regard as the benefits of having a mentor? 'Access to information I would not otherwise have had; the support to make the best use of that information; guidance; and, how best to focus to achieve your highest aims.'

REFLECTIVE ACTIONS

- How will you manage the database?
- How will you ensure ongoing support and development for both mentors and mentees?
- What other resources can you use to support the scheme?
- How will you ensure pitfalls are kept to a minimum?

Chapter Five
The role of mentoring in diversity and culture

'It's not our differences that divide us; it's our judgements about each other that do' wrote Meg Wheatley (2002). These judgements are not so much cultural as part of our mental models or mindsets, both of which we have already discussed. Just to recap, we can describe mindsets or mental models as the filters through which people view the world, themselves and others. People can unconsciously discriminate because these mindsets operate below consciousness.

The potential for prejudice is present when we hold a stereotype about a group that is incongruent with the attributes we believe are required for a role. People's subjective interpretation of a person or group may lead them to believe that these individuals do not 'have what it takes' and therefore dismiss them, making people feel invisible with no voice. In today's world, this is no longer acceptable.

Diversity

Today, companies work within a global marketplace that often requires working across national boundaries and cultures. Yet more than half of those who are given international assignments return early, disappointed, either disliking the role or unable to adjust to a different country. Dealing with diversity is a reality most organizations today have to deal with and the skills required are not those that are taught on training courses. These skills are described as building trust through 'emotionally connecting with people from different backgrounds' (Joplin and Daus, 1997) – what has been called 'relationship competence'. The GLOBE study found agreement across 62 nations that people wanted leaders they described as 'encouraging, positive, motivational, confidence builder, dynamic and [with] foresight' (Den Harytog *et al*, 1999). Having an open mind and positive attitude is therefore required wherever you are in the world and mentors who fit this are needed to guide others towards these traits.

The second attribute required for working with diversity is individuals who are open to new experiences, sometimes called 'unbridled inquisitiveness' (Gregerson *et al*, 1998). For companies across the United States, Japan and Europe, those who were looking for people able to work in diverse cultures regarded openness to new cultures as important as technical skills.

At Zurich Financial Services managers are often asked to work across Europe, including the UK and Ireland. Mentoring has been a really effective way to address cultural issues.

CASE STUDY   Zurich Insurance Germany

In 2009, a mentoring scheme was set up as a pilot at Zurich Insurance in Germany to support management capabilities. The idea had been suggested in their first Employee Engagement Survey and the response was positive, so the first 16 people to participate were signed up. This included mentors and mentees. The team responsible for the scheme were Hajo Bruggemann, Head of Talent Management, and Sabine Bechler.

Participation in the mentoring programme was on a voluntary basis. Mentors tended to be in the top 100 management of Zurich Germany, while mentees were those who had one to three years' experience in first-line management. They became known as the 'TandemZ' and the programme was monitored for 12 months.

Jahwed volunteered to be a mentee as he had benefited from mentors while at school and wanted to discuss topics with a more experienced mentor. Scanning the short profiles of mentors, Jahwed chose a woman he knew by reputation and he felt a woman would provide a different perspective and decision-making process. He described the benefits of the mentoring relationship:

> It has given me access to higher management and an understanding of topics and issues they have to deal with. Something I would have never have known. It also provided support to my career, opening doors, and to networks.

Before starting the programme, mentees had to define what they expected to learn or discuss during the sessions, which tended to be bimonthly. Topics included management issues, projects, knowledge, methods, career and competence, as well as company values and culture. Other issues were also included on a lesser basis, such as intercultural and interdepartmental cooperation, or more personal issues, such as work–life balance. Often, mentors served as a 'sounding board' to the mentees to test new ideas.

Sophia also volunteered to be a mentee after her role expanded and her line manager suggested a mentor would be helpful. She said:

> I had joined the company in 1992 and now I was leading four teams made up of about 60 people in total. I was offered a choice from three mentors whose profiles I studied that were quite personal. I chose one that seemed to be like me. Similar to me, the mentor was empathetic and felt things. Since starting the mentoring relationship I have gained self-confidence, motivation and expanded my competencies. It was great to talk to a mentor. You learn so much about yourself with the feedback and how command structures work.

What has transpired is clear evidence that mentees gain insight into the work of senior management and the formal and informal rules while at the same time they establish internal networks to aid their career. In fact, the ultimate goal was for the mentee to be encouraged to pursue his or her own career.

Hajo Bruggemann put himself forward as a mentor because he not only had many years with the company, but had worked in three different regional offices in Germany and understood regional differences. These days he is engaged in international projects dealing with different cultures and perspectives.

As a mentor Hajo said:

> You get déjà vu experiences which you can't remember at first until you work with a mentee and remember. You suddenly see yourself as the mentee and feel the same feelings as years ago, facing the same issues. The difference now is you can reflect on the decisions you took, so you have lots of empathy combined with wisdom. I try not to give advice or tell them what to do but ask questions. In an open discussion, you let the mentee come to their own conclusion. It's hard though with those déjà vu experiences.

The scheme was set up because one of the findings from an employee survey was that the company should do more for managers facing different situations – especially young managers. Following a restructuring of the company people had to do more with less and international work became more important. For many, shifting from a local view of the business to a global view was difficult, and so help was needed.

'The company works within nine different cultures across Europe which can be either enriching or tortuous,' said Hajo, 'and as Head of Talent Management I wanted us to find the best way to provide that help.'

I asked if the mentors had received any training and was told that there wasn't formal training but instead a day was held where guidelines were set and it was explained clearly how mentoring differed from coaching. The pilot has now been completed and evaluated. The results were so good a slogan has developed to sum up the programme: Experience, Trust, Appreciation.

Hans-Joachim Brueggemann concludes:

> TandemZ is an ideal tool to establish a culture where knowledge and experience is passed on from senior to junior management. This helps us create a competence network throughout the group, at the same time strengthening the position of our senior management as role models. We have therefore decided to

establish the mentoring program as a fixed item on our leadership development agenda.'

The scheme is now expanding. In Ireland, the Chief Executive could see the benefits and has in fact started with himself as a mentor to three mentees, passing on his wisdom and knowledge. It also enables him to get 'close to the floor'.

The scheme at Zurich has been a cost-effective way to develop people – both mentors and mentees. For this reason it is going to be extended and expanded. It also fits with their commitment to the European 70:20:10 model of learning based on research, which showed that between 70 and 90 per cent of learning occurs as part of normal work rather than through off-job training courses. The model states that:

- 70 per cent of workplace learning is through on-the-job experiences and practice;
- 20 per cent of workplace learning is through mentoring, networking and learning from others;
- 10 per cent of workplace learning is through formal training or seminars.

Mentoring has enabled this company to work across cultural boundaries in an effective way. But there is another diversity challenge that is slow to be addressed. Can mentoring help this one?

Gender

A far reaching effect of diversity is gender. In August 2010 Lord Mervyn Davies was appointed to look into the problem of why there are so few women at the top of UK boardrooms. The coalition government of the day announced that only 12 per cent (139) of FTSE 100 company directors were women. Upon a closer inspection, the reality is actually worse. Many of these women are on the boards of more than one company, leaving

120 women out of 1,110 directors. Many are not UK nationals, several being American, and then there are a handful of women with titles such as Baroness.

In addition, of the 120 women, only 20 of them (6 per cent) hold the position of executive director and run the company on a daily basis, compared to 309 male equivalents. More than one-fifth of FTSE companies have no female directors at board level. There has been some progress in the last few years but the pace of progress has been very slow. In fact the Equality and Human Rights Commission estimates that it will take another 73 years before equal numbers of women and men are represented in the FTSE 100 boardrooms. That estimation is rather optimistic as some companies are reporting fewer women in senior management than a few years ago.

The situation is worse in the FTSE 250 companies today (those ranked 101 to 350), with 54 per cent having no female directors. The Equality and Human Rights Commission estimate that it won't be until 2225 that equal numbers will be reached in all the UK boardrooms. Why has it been so difficult to have equal representation in our organizations?

In 2001, Catalyst, the US research organization, found the biggest barrier to the advancement of women as reported by women was a lack of mentoring opportunities. Third on the list of barriers was exclusion from informal networks, followed by lack of female role models. These are issues mentoring can address. In my own research with women board directors in the UK it was found that while there was a lack of role models, having someone believe in their capabilities and potential early on who can act as a guide to their career had been a fundamental part of their development. It was interesting to also find that those who had someone take an interest in them early on were more likely to act as a mentor for other women. Those who had 'made it on their own' were more likely to hold the view of 'I did it alone so those coming up can do the same.'

In an age where over half of undergraduates are women we need to attract women to senior roles and therefore the issue of gender and mentoring has to be addressed.

Research appears to identify four main barriers to women progressing through to senior roles. The first is the belief by some that all that is required is time and women will 'break through'. However, if we explore how long it is taking for the number women on boards to increase it becomes clear that progress is so slow that it will take decades before there is fair representation. What we know is that social change does not move forward without struggle and conflict. As women gain greater equality, a portion of people react against it. There are now signs of a halt to progress and this is reflected in the fact that the number of women in senior roles within organizations is decreasing. Some believe such progress has reached its limit while women still carry out most of the home and family duties, coupled with employer policies and a structure of work that favours those who do not have the responsibility for child rearing.

The second barrier is the belief by some that there are too few capable women for the role. Yet when this issue is raised most women in senior posts disagree and in fact the evidence seems to suggest that women are performing better on the 360 degree feedback of leadership programmes than their male colleagues. Exploring this barrier further we find that it actually covers up a mix of beliefs, including unease that women in senior roles would 'upset' the familiarity of senior networks. Many are also concerned that a female director will have a 'woman's agenda', putting pressure on those few who do succeed to close the door behind them.

The challenge, it seems, is to make a paradigm shift from regarding one model of leader to many models, including the natural way women lead. Studies over decades clearly show that people associate women and men with different traits. Women tend to be associated with qualities such as caring, helpful, kind and sympathetic. While in contrast, men are associated with qualities such as strong, ambitious, dominant, self-confident and forceful. These latter traits are also those many people associate with a leader in what is known as an 'implicit leadership theory'.

In my own research with schools, girls as young as 7 described leadership as 'being helpful, being nice, not being bossy', while boys of the same age described leadership as 'having courage, being strong or brave and having belief in yourself' (Owen, 2007). When girls took leadership roles the boys labelled them 'bossy'. As a result of this many girls shy away from leadership because they regard being bossy as a negative stereotype for themselves. In the workplace a female executive of a global company remarked: 'People often have to speak up to defend their turf, but when women did so, they were vilified. They were labelled "control freaks"; while men acting the same way were called "passionate"' (Early and Carla, 2007). Women are caught in a difficult situation – they have to demonstrate both female and male traits to be accepted. So is there a distinct leadership style for women acceptable by society?

Perhaps the most comprehensive study on the way women lead was done by Judy Rosener, who described women's leadership as:

- linking rather than ranking people;
- favouring interactive, collaborative leadership styles;
- sustaining fruitful collaborations;
- comfortably sharing information and power;
- seeing distribution of power as victory, not surrender;
- readily accepting and dealing with ambiguity;
- honouring intuition as well as rationality;
- appreciating cultural diversity.

In today's environment this style of leadership is more important than ever to deal with a fast-changing world. With cuts in public services the need for partnerships and collaborative leadership is vital, as is the ability to deal with ambiguity.

More recently, researchers used a framework developed by James McGregor Burns that distinguishes transformational and transactional leadership. Transformational leaders establish themselves as role models by gaining followers' trust and confidence. They state future goals and innovate even in very successful organizations. These leaders mentor and empower followers, encouraging them to develop their full potential, resulting in them contributing more effectively in their organizations. In contrast, transactional leaders establish give-and-take relationships that appeal to subordinates' self-interest. Such leaders manage in the conventional manner of clarifying subordinates' responsibilities, rewarding them for meeting objectives and correcting them if they do not. While both styles are different, most leaders adopt some behaviours from both types.

These and other researchers found that, in general, female leaders were more transformational than male peers, especially when it came to giving support and encouragement to subordinates. They also engaged in more of the rewarding behaviours that are one aspect of transactional leadership. Whereas, male leaders exceeded on aspects of transactional leadership involving disciplinary and corrective actions. They were also more likely to be laissez-faire leaders, who take little responsibility for managing. It is interesting to note that the transformational style is more suited to leading organizations today. The research shows not only the different ways men and women lead but that what is needed is more transformational leadership and that this will be achieved with more women in leadership roles. All of which has huge implications for mentoring.

The third barrier to women progressing is the belief that women are not interested in senior roles. It is true that women as a rule don't tend to promote and push themselves forward as some men may, preferring to be asked instead. It's just that women have a different approach. Whereas some men will have their successor in mind after six months in a role, women tend to focus more on doing a good job. It is differences like this between the sexes that need to be understood and valued.

Others will say women prefer to stay in supervisory roles. There are of course those who are more comfortable in these roles, just as many of their male colleagues are, but this is not the case for many others, as shown by the research from Catalyst, which found that female executives were just as likely to aspire to the top job as male colleagues but that women endure barriers to their advancement not experienced by men. Therefore it is wrong to assume the majority of capable women do not wish to reach the top of their profession.

In a study of a large law firms, it was found that women were no less likely than men to begin their career at such firms but more likely to leave them for roles in the public sector or corporate sector. The reasons for their departure were because of family commitments. For the women that stayed, 60 per cent had no children and the minority who did waited until they were at partner level before doing so. Women need flexibility. But the trade off is their ability to be leaders. At present we appear to recognize women's rights but ignore women's strengths.

Finally, the last barrier is that some employers will say they can't find women to be included in the pool of candidates for promotion. However, many of their male counterparts who are put forward are clearly not capable at that time in their career and this needs to be acknowledged. So why does the pool of women decline as leadership roles become more demanding? It's been found that promotion comes more slowly for women than for men with the same qualifications. At the same time, new research has found that there isn't so much a glass ceiling as a labyrinth of challenges throughout women's careers that men do not have to endure. By the time many women reach 40 they are giving up. Action needs to be taken to address this loss of talent.

CASE STUDY   The FTSE 100 cross-company mentoring programme

In the UK a scheme has now been introduced to try and increase the number of women in strategic decision-making bodies, including corporate boards. The FTSE 100 Cross-Company Mentoring Programme brings together chairpersons and CEOs and those who influence decisions about board appointments with senior executive women showing potential for board membership. The chairs and CEOs mentor these women to the point where they will be credible candidates for executive and non-executive directorships and other top leadership roles. So far, 62 women have been mentored on the scheme since 2003 and 54 of them have achieved a significant appointment or promotion.

The scheme currently has 39 mentors and 30 mentees. 'Have the confidence to be yourself' was the advice the Chair of Shell gave his mentee on the scheme.

How does it work?

When a company joins the scheme its chair becomes a mentor. The mentees do not come from the mentor's organization, so there is no 'favouritism'. Since the start of the scheme, mentors of non-FTSE organizations have also been made welcome. Each organization pays a subscription to join that covers the costs of administrating the scheme. When a FTSE 100 company joins the scheme the chair is made a mentor and they nominate as a mentee the woman having the highest potential from just below board level. Each mentee is 'matched' with a mentor from a different organization. The mentoring pairs work together for a year to two years, meeting regularly. Some mentors give mentees a project or piece of work that enables the development of the mentee. Mentors are often generous with their contacts and network and act as sponsors.

Director of the FTSE scheme Peninah Thomson sums it up by saying 'What mentors can do is to help women interpret the dominant culture' (Thomson, 2010). Offshoots of the scheme are now running in other countries, including France. Veronique Preaux-Cobti is co-director of Board Women Partners and explains one of the barriers in practice: 'Initially our chairman said they were not against nominating women to boards but they didn't know any with the required profile,' she recalls. 'We said we won't find any if you look for women who have the same profile as men' (*Financial Times*, 2010). This demonstrates the pressure on women to be like a man and not themselves in the corporate world. What boards need is fresh thinking, different ideas and perspectives and more transformational leadership.

Herminia Ibarra, a Professor at Insead Business School, explains 'If you ask women to be inauthentic, they lose value. They need to figure out how to make the system work for them' (*Financial Times*, 2010). The need for female mentors as well as male mentors is also growing, and not just for top roles.

My own study of women on FTSE boards has some interesting findings and includes 'advice' to other women from the women I interviewed. It was a small study of ten women because it was a qualitative analysis based on lengthy interviews. Out of the ten, two had received some kind of mentoring in their career. Yet the impact was huge. 'The company's first personnel officer picked me out and showed me how to better myself. I would never have come this far if she hadn't done that. After that, male colleagues helped and I took on their positive attributes.' The second director said 'I had two! Both were my boss and male. They challenged me to be more confident and have higher aspirations, broaden my skills and take on ambitious projects. They both gave me constructive encouragement, time and management education.'

Amongst the ten were also two women whose attitudes were that because they didn't have any support they shouldn't give any to anyone else, and would not be interested in being a mentor. Their comments were similar: 'Get on with it and don't worry about being female' and 'Think about being a director and stop thinking of being a woman.' Can you imagine someone saying to a man 'Don't think about being a man'? The other eight all said they would enjoy mentoring others. When asked what advice they would give other women who had the aspiration of becoming a FTSE director they said:

> Don't be reticent about taking on new things or moving into new areas – women underestimate their abilities. So believe in yourself and take risks – men don't worry about this.

> Why do you want to be a director? It's less meaningful than you expect. Don't aspire to be a director for the sake of it. Ask what you can contribute and use the influence it gives you. Study finance and statutory issues, as these are discussed a lot. Think about presentation and speaking with authority. Network – the outside environment is talked about, so it's helpful. Have mixed as well as female networks.

> Keep a sense of humour. Be good at your job and don't be threatened by colleagues. Be better at politics to get the business objectives achieved.

> Become financially literate – it's discussed at board level more than anything else. Be sure you're climbing the right ladder – there's a danger if it's too specialist such as HR or IT. Think politically, women are too open. I think men should change but we have to work with them for now.

> Recognize it's a 100 per cent role and uncompromising. You have to compete and keep on the ladder. You can't have long-term career breaks to keep up.

> Think strategically, be in the right place at the right time. Don't make it an issue that you are female. Men have to feel comfortable with you.

> Be very focused, don't be one of the pack, stand out and be prepared to go it alone. Persist and don't take things personally. Be resilient. Listen and be a people person.

> Be clear about your strengths and weaknesses, play to your strengths and build a team to compensate for your weaknesses. Ask 'Do my values fit here?' You'll be happier if they do, and successful.

These comments are not only good advice but show what life is like as a board director. Yet progress is still painfully slow in the UK. This contrasts with a much faster pace in France, where the threat of draft legislation was based on reserving 40 per cent of board members for women. Mentoring is an important tool for women in their bid to advance their careers. Male managers tend to have informal networks that provide contacts, feedback and career advice, whether it's at the golf club, the local pub or in an executive stand to watch their favourite football team.

Today organizations need to build a talent pipeline of more diverse leaders, who may not be identified through the traditional processes. In some cases mentors for this will need to come from outside the organization. This is because women and ethnic minorities who are looking for a mentor at a senior level still have to choose mentors who are mostly white and male. In an American study it was found that the difficulty of finding mentors who are of colour was a huge barrier to success. At the same time, successful women and those from ethnic backgrounds are reticent to come forward as a mentor because they are worried about appearing to 'favour' other women or minorities. The solution is for mentoring to become part of what executives do in their day-to-day job. So far, the barriers discussed here have been external but there are internal barriers too.

In 2002 research from the University of California (Hoyt 2002) explored gender and self-efficacy and found that negative stereotypes undermined the individual's assessment of their abilities and resulted in decreased performance that can be self-threatening. If persistent stereotype threat occurs individuals may disengage from that domain and this may be why we hear so many girls and women say they are not a leader and display 'disidentification' with the role. The research found that leadership self-efficacy moderated the effect of stereotype threat. Where this work becomes unique is that the researcher believed stereotype activation may actually be empowering to women with high leadership self-efficacy. In fact they will perceive the stereotype as challenging whereas women with low leadership self-efficacy will feel threatened and so it has the opposite effect depending on the leadership self-efficacy of the woman. This explains why a handful of women do break through the barriers.

This cognitive appraisal of a leadership situation seems to affect more females because of stereotyping that perceives leadership as 'bossy' and not the right image for a girl or woman. As a result it's been found that a woman with low leadership self-efficacy is more likely to perform poorly as a group leader, be more anxious prior to leading a group, and identify less with the leadership role. Therefore negative stereotyping has an effect on women, but depending on their leadership self-efficacy will be either a challenge or a threat. It was also found that for men, the benefits of gaining a high rank in the hierarchy was more of an influencer in putting themselves forward for leadership than belief in their capabilities.

There is no doubt that self-efficacy and stereotyping affect women far more than men. The pattern that seems to be emerging is that gender role identity and not just gender is a critical factor for leadership and that this role identity not only influences whether women believe they are a leader but also causes some to actually avoid leadership roles so they don't practise and learn it. Imagine the implications of this for leadership learning and development within organizations.

Another study also found that gender itself wasn't the key factor so much as the individual's gender role identity. A girl or woman who perceives herself as strong and competitive, ie has masculine-type behaviours as well as female behaviours incorporated into her self-concept, is more likely to engage in leadership activities and so develop higher leadership self-efficacy.

Therefore gender-role socialization can constrain women in developing leadership self-efficacy, which results in a narrowing of their occupational choices. It is lack of self-efficacy and confidence that is limiting their lives as much as prejudice and organizational barriers and cultures. Mentors need to understand how to develop leadership efficacy if more women are to succeed in more leadership roles. It will also improve mentoring in organizations and as the message coming out of this manual is that mentors gain as much from a mentoring process as their mentees, having more women involved as mentors also is an excellent way for people to develop.

REFLECTIVE ACTIONS

- Is culture an issue the mentoring scheme needs to address?
- How can the mentoring scheme help?
- How can you develop mentors who understand the diversity issues?
- What can you do to enable the mentor to address gender challenges?

Chapter Six
Evaluating mentoring

Evaluating any learning is challenging, because we are complex beings and implicit knowledge is not recognized until it becomes explicit. However, having a mentoring scheme in an organization will require evaluation. Therefore, this chapter will try to give some practical help with evaluation. If the process follows what has already been suggested at the pre-programme stage it will be easier.

The terminology

The science of evaluation has its own language, so some of the terminology will be explained where necessary, to ensure correct understanding. The cost and effectiveness of any scheme are separate measures of the input and the output of that scheme, thus enabling decisions to be taken. For example, if two different programmes produce equally effective results, then the less costly one will be preferred. Therefore the emphasis is on putting a specific value on the input or output. If both input and output can be measured in monetary terms then cost–benefit can be used.

Today, the quest is to demonstrate value to the organization and customer. The value of a mentoring scheme is based on how it contributes to the success of the organization. This is why it is important at the start to be clear and state why the scheme was initiated. Was it to improve performance, retain quality people or enable individuals to use more initiative and lead difficult projects? What is clear, is that a mentoring scheme should add greater value than it costs and rarely result in lost production time.

What is required to evaluate a mentoring scheme is information that can be used to measure its value. Therefore it is important to ask whether the measures are:

- reliable – the measures consistently show the same results under similar circumstances;
- valid – the measures accurately measure what they were intended to do;
- general – the results of the measures can be compared.

Do not expect a single measure to provide data to base decisions on. There are many variables that will have an impact, such as how good the mentor is or how the mentee is influenced by the organization. The key is to keep focused on why the scheme was set up in the first place.

The evaluation plan

The plan begins with a question: what do we want to know about the impact of our mentoring process on the organization? Then you can follow a step-by-step approach.

Step 1: What outcomes are you getting from other interventions, training programmes, organization development initiatives?

Once clear of this you begin with what you already know. You can call these your baseline indicators and they will include management development, culture change, executive development, diversity programmes and technical skills training. How are these fulfilling the organizational and learning development objectives?

This can include numbers, such as how many people participate each year, the duration of programmes as well as the cost.

Step 2: Which of the following do you expect to have an impact from the mentoring scheme?

- Recruitment;
- retention;
- succession planning;
- skills;
- greater responsibility;
- leadership;
- better ideas and improved understanding of issues;
- reduction in stress levels;
- greater confidence and decision making;
- improved relationships and communication between colleagues;
- change achieved more easily;
- motivation of mentees;
- motivation of mentors;
- costs of development;
- customer/public image.

Once the baselines are built you can decide which you can use to evaluate the mentoring process.

Step 3: Set up a way of tracking the mentees

This might include their:

- profiles and current role;
- skills at the start of the mentoring process;
- launch dates;
- planned objectives;
- time spent on development;
- costs for time away from day job and keeping record of development.

Using this method it is possible to show how much skills and performance have increased. You should then include a way of tracking the career progress of the mentee.

Step 4: Use baseline information to also record the effectiveness of the mentor

This can begin with simple questions such as: Do you believe you have the knowledge and skills to be a successful mentor? What are these? Are you clear about the mentoring process? Also include their:

- attitude and loyalty towards the organization;
- career plans;
- time they can invest in mentoring;
- expectations from mentoring.

All this baseline information, along with other data, will enable you to make a good assessment of the cost effectiveness of the mentoring scheme you are setting up.

Step 5: The final cost

The final cost is that of the support, administration and team who will oversee the mentoring scheme. Therefore establish a database for recording these costs while also ensuring a simple reporting process for both mentors and mentees at regular intervals.

Why evaluate?

Throughout the evaluation process it is important to ask: What is the purpose of evaluation? You may come up with different answers such as to justify the cost to the budget holders or to show that it is contributing to achieving the objectives of the business. These are all relevant but the most important answer is to improve the mentoring process for the benefit of all the stakeholders. Mentoring is not static or a quick fix. As part of a social structure it is dynamic and constantly shifting. Evaluation isn't about measuring a fixed point in time to justify itself but rather to seek actions that can be taken to enhance and improve it.

CASE STUDY Shell International Exploration and Production

I first worked with this part of Shell in the 1990s, when they were trying new ideas in the area of personal development. In 1997, the division for research and technical services introduced mentoring. While mentoring had already been used in the company, this was the first time the focus was on personal development. In this division, where the focus was on cutting-edge research and technological consultancy, the structure was team based with only two layers of hierarchy: the management committee and teams. Responsibility for budgets and strategy was handled within the teams, which included new graduates. Therefore taking responsibility early on was the norm.

While the senior management supported the scheme, they wanted to control the process of finding mentors and matching them with graduates. This acted as a block in an environment where responsibility and self-management was the norm. The mentees were suspicious of the control, while the senior managers took this as apathy. It was deadlock and nothing happened for months. They needed to look again at what they were trying to achieve and how they were going to achieve it.

The aim of the mentoring scheme was to develop the graduates and they wanted to decide for themselves if mentoring was a way they wanted to explore. At the same time, mentors should have a say in who they mentor. Therefore, the scheme was changed to treat both groups as adults who could decide this for themselves. Now mentors nominate themselves and put their curriculum vitae into a database. Graduate mentees work through the database to decide who they would like to mentor them, meeting them face to face before making a final decision. Mentors are allowed to take up to three mentees.

Removing controls and treating both mentors and mentees as responsible adults resulted in an active mentoring scheme based on openness and trust, with all graduates participating. Once it began to flow a person was appointed to promote, communicate, monitor and support the scheme. Every mentee is interviewed to ensure they understand the scheme. The mentors have a coach and each has to go through a learning process before they begin.

When evaluated by external people, it was found that giving the graduates the ability to choose their own mentors was fundamental to its success. So, while the first effort didn't work, having the courage to address the scheme according to the culture of the organization, resulted in success. This demonstrates why evaluation is so important and why you need to decide how you will evaluate a scheme before it begins.

The logic model

Another way of evaluating is to use a more formal process. One that can be used is called the 'logic model'. Here the model describes logical linkages among and between resources, activities, outputs, participants and outcomes that are short, intermediate and long term, and related to the specific situation/purpose. A mentoring process designed with assessment in mind is much more likely to provide beneficial data.

Building the logic model can begin by asking the following questions:

- What is the current situation that we intend to have an impact on (the purpose of setting up a mentoring scheme)?
- What will it look like when we achieve the desired outcome?
- What behaviours need to change for that outcome to be achieved?
- What knowledge or skills do people need before the behaviour will change?
- What actions are required to enable the necessary learning?
- What resources (including support) will be required to achieve the desired outcome?

It acknowledges that this is a linear model to simulate a multi-dimensional process but the goal is to keep it simple and therefore effective. Someone who has developed logic models is Howard Ladewig. According to Ladewig, there are certain characteristics of schemes and programmes that enable others to value and support them. By describing the characteristics of the mentoring system that demonstrate *relevance, quality and impact*, Ladewig states it fosters buy-in from all the stakeholders.

Let's build the model up (Figure 6.1). In each box are the things to consider.

FIGURE 6.1

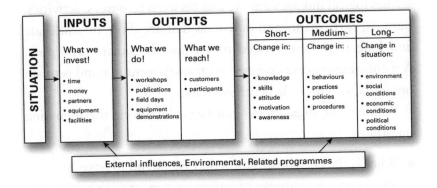

The situation

A statement of the situation provides an opportunity to communicate the *relevance* of the mentoring process and can include:

- a statement of the problem – the causes and symptoms and their effect on the organization;

- an assessment of the likely consequences if nothing is done to change this, including the costs;

- a description of who and what is affected by the problem;

- the stakeholders; who is affected; what other interventions are trying to address the problem.

The situation statement will provide a baseline for comparison at intervals and the end of the scheme. By describing the problem and the symptoms it becomes possible to determine whether change has occurred. Describing who is affected by the problem allows assessment of who has benefited.

Inputs

These include what we invest into the scheme, such as:

- time invested by mentors, managers and mentees;
- fiscal resources;
- facilities and equipment;
- training, materials, research;
- involvement of collaborators in the planning, delivery and evaluation of the scheme.

Here you are communicating the *quality* of the scheme. Also, when the planned inputs are described, assessing their effectiveness is made easier. If a comparison of actual with planned investment is included, the evaluation can justify budgets and be used to improve future schemes.

Outputs

These are the things we do in the mentoring scheme and the people it reaches. Describing the outputs shows the linkages with the situation that is being addressed (eg succession planning) and the *impact* of the scheme (intended outcomes). This can include:

- creating a database;
- development and support for mentors;
- preparing mentees;
- developing resource materials.

At the centre of the model are the people the scheme reaches. They are the bridge between the situation and the impact. Information about them can include:

- their characteristics and behaviours;
- the number in a target group that were reached;

- their learning objectives;
- the number of mentoring sessions they attended;
- the level of satisfaction participants express for the scheme.

Outcomes

These are the short-term, intermediate and long-term outcomes that answer the question 'What happened as a result of the scheme?' Short-term outcomes can include changes in:

- awareness of the scheme and its purpose;
- the knowledge and skills needed to ensure a successful scheme and how it impacts on the situation to be resolved;
- the motivation of employees to effect the desired changes;
- the attitude of those participating and the belief that they can make a difference.

Intermediate outcomes follow on from the short-term outcomes such as:

- behaviours exhibited by participants in the scheme;
- impact on their work areas and the people around them.

Long-term outcomes are the changes in behaviours that result in changed organizational impact such as:

- improved culture or increased income;
- improved sustainable growth of the organization;
- the right leadership.

Evaluation planning

To assess the scheme an evaluation plan can be superimposed using the logic model format.

- Were specific inputs made as planned in terms of the amount of input, timing and quality of input?
- Were the desired number of participants and level of participation achieved?
- Were specific actions carried out as planned in terms of timing, content and quality?
- What indicators were identified for short-, medium- and long-term outcomes?
- Did participants demonstrate the desired level of knowledge increase, enhanced awareness and/or motivation?
- Did management practices and behaviours improve as expected from the mentoring scheme?

FIGURE 6.2   Insertion of evaluation plan into the logic model

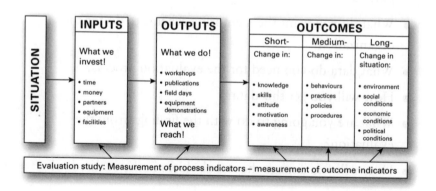

Final recommendations are that developing the appropriate and measurable indicators during the planning phase is the key to a good evaluation. It also enables the project team to identify

what baseline data may be available to help evaluate the scheme or design a process to collect baseline data before the scheme is launched. Indicators to measure behavioural changes should specify which behaviours and skills are targeted by the process.

The best evaluation is always done with the participation of all the stakeholders engaged in the process, whereby learning is also part of the evaluation that goes beyond numbers. This needs to be explained to and seen by all, so that best practice will emerge. Evaluation then has the capability to enhance the practice of the mentors, mentees, line managers, support team and executive while they are being evaluated.

What is set out here is an attempt to offer the most effective way for understanding the impact of mentoring in different contexts while ensuring the process itself and those involved regard it as additional learning.

REFLECTIVE AND ACTION NOTES

- Why did you set up a mentoring scheme – what was its purpose?
- What do you want the mentoring scheme to do for the organization?
- What data do you need for the evaluation process?
- How will you get this data?
- What are you going to do with the findings from the evaluation?
- How will you engage the stakeholders in the evaluation?

Chapter Seven
The wisdom of mentoring

So far we have focused on order and process: a management approach to setting up a mentoring scheme in your organization. It is now time to move beyond management processes and bring a leadership approach. To ensure a truly successful mentoring scheme you are required to use your leadership and this means questioning and challenging and most of all transforming people and the organization while taking people with you. To achieve this, it is important to understand the latest knowledge of two of the key elements required for mentoring:

- the sharing of wisdom; and,

- why as human beings we find change so difficult.

At the start of the book I included a quote from a senior adviser from the United Nations. It is now time to elaborate this and go deeper into the purpose and requirements of mentoring than we have done so far. First, the quote included at the start of this book:

> I've dealt with many different problems around the world, and I've concluded that there's only one real problem: over the past one hundred years, the power that technology has given us has grown beyond anyone's wildest imagination, but our wisdom has not. If the gap between our power and our wisdom is not redressed soon, I don't have much hope for our prospects.
>
> (Senge *et al*, 2005: 187)

Can mentoring close the gap? I believe it can if we take it beyond a Human Resources process issue and give it a broader context and purpose. If mentoring can develop wisdom in organizations it will enable us to cope with any crisis. If we can replace greed and ego – which has resulted in corporate fraud, incompetence at board level and the global banking crisis – we can use the wisdom of each person in every organization to close the gap between power and wisdom. This is where mentoring is so important and so very different from coaching. First let's try to understand the concept of wisdom.

Understanding wisdom

Wisdom is defined as 'good judgement and advice in difficult and uncertain matters of life'. It is also defined in dictionaries as 'insight and knowledge about oneself and the world'. In the field of psychology, where the definition includes those individuals with high levels of moral reasoning, teams of people in different parts of the world have been trying to get an even deeper understanding of not just what wisdom is, but how it is practised and why some people seem to have wisdom and others not.

In one study by psychologists Pasupathi and Staudinger (2001), they found moral reasoning was indeed associated with wisdom-related performance. Meanwhile the 'Berlin Group' found that wisdom appears to be a cognitive domain in adulthood that does not seem to have an advantage such as age or the group but rather reflects individual and specific life experiences. Kunzmann and Baltes (2005) go on to argue that it is not specific competencies that distinguish wisdom from other competencies such as emotional intelligence or creativity, but it's the way in which such elements interact as wisdom that is unique. They describe this interaction as an 'integrative and holistic' approach towards challenges and life in general that embraces the past, present and future. The interaction also takes into account contextual differences while addressing the uncertainties in making sense of the past, present and future.

In Austria, Judith Gluck and Susan Bluck (2004) have asked the question: why do certain individuals develop high levels of wisdom in the course of their lives, while others do not? As a result they have developed the MORE Wisdom model that relates to the four key skills they have been testing. These are: Mastery, Openness to experience, a Reflective attitude, and Emotion regulation skills. They found that people who develop wisdom use these resources when approaching challenges, and by using them, they develop even further. These are the skills required in mentors. Remember when we looked at diversity, it was people who had the ability to be open to different experiences that were an asset to organizations that work across national boundaries. These are skills that can be developed through mentoring and continued through reflection as skills individuals can develop throughout their lives. It also enables people to become excellent mentors, who in turn can mentor others.

A deeper understanding of wisdom comes from sociologist Monika Ardelt based in the United States. Unlike the previous researchers who regarded wisdom as a system of expert knowledge, Ardelt regards wisdom as a 'combination of personality qualities that cannot exist independently of individuals' (2005). Her model of wisdom is based on three-dimensional personalities consisting of Cognitive, Reflective and Affective. Her research found that those who scored high on wisdom were more reflective and used more active coping strategies. This is another reason why reflection is so important in the mentoring process.

Ardelt argues that while much is written about explicit theories of wisdom, people have implicit theories based on her model. She shows that even culture affects implicit theories; for example, those living in Western cultures emphasize the cognitive aspects of wisdom, whereas people living in Eastern cultures emphasize both the cognitive and affective dimensions. Her model is based on the three elements below working together. To help you, check the model against the purpose and aims of why you are setting up or running a mentoring scheme. Also ask whether mentors are developing these skills in their development work before acting as mentors.

Cognitive – an understanding of life and a desire to know the truth that includes knowledge, the acceptance of the positive and negative aspects of human beings, the limits of knowledge and uncertainties. This, in practice, includes the ability and willingness to understand a situation, and an acknowledgement of ambiguity and uncertainty in life.

Reflective – the perception of things from multiple perspectives that requires self-examination, self-awareness and insight. In practice this means the absence of subjectivity and projection, in other words the tendency to blame other people or circumstances for one's own situation or feelings.

Affective – sympathy, love and compassion for others. In practice this requires positive emotions and behaviour towards others and the absence of indifference.

Mentoring is a way of developing this wisdom, for, as Ardelt states, 'a deep and unbiased understanding of life is only possible after one has "seen through illusion" and transcended one's subjectivity and projections to perceive reality as it is'. Having the time to reflect and gain different perspectives with a mentor while becoming more self-aware, a mentee can see and accept the reality of the present and gain better understanding of oneself and others in a work situation. The outcome should be to shift from self-centredness to compassion and understanding of others. This is indeed the development of wisdom in action brought about by good mentoring.

By examining these latest ideas and integrating them into a mentoring system the outcome will not only be superb mentoring but a mentoring system fit for the 21st century.

Can we all be wise?

Not everyone will benefit from mentoring and some of the reasons need to be addressed with a way forward that can help. Most of these barriers are at a cognitive level but what will become clear is that emotions such as fear and anxiety are also often involved. Let's begin with asking you some questions.

- If you had to choose, would you take lots of success and validation – or lots of challenge?

- When do you feel smartest – after an outstanding performance or after you've just learned something challenging?

- Do you believe that you can learn new things but not really change how intelligent you are?

These alternatives exemplify either a 'fixed' or 'growth' mindset according to Carol Dweck (2006). For someone to be a good mentor or mentee they really do need to have a growth mindset. This means they assume people can improve in just about any area of their life through learning and practice. A growth mindset is open to learning from feedback, willing to risk and enjoy challenges and accepts one's strengths and weaknesses. A growth mindset also means a person appreciates others' capabilities, doesn't feel threatened in the face of frustration and strives to improve in new domains in their life.

In contrast, those with a fixed mindset assume that ability is a fixed quality and is revealed in performance. They focus on looking good and as such tend to see new endeavours as threatening and give up more quickly when frustrated. People with a fixed mindset will avoid activities they don't think they are good at and will insulate themselves from negative evaluation.

In Boorstin's book *The Discoverers* (1985) he asserts that the primary barrier to progress is not ignorance but the illusion of knowledge and expertise. Unfortunately, the fixed mindset may be over-represented in management positions and is usually recognized as a person more eager to look good than learn. A good mentor will enable those with a fixed mindset to become aware of their inner mindset 'voice' through reflective practice and bring to the surface the fixed mindset beliefs. Once on the surface a good mentor can help them talk back to these beliefs with a growth mindset.

Mentoring in the 21st century can revert back to its original meaning to take it beyond what to do, to 'how to be'. Robert Bly in *The Sibling Society* (1996) describes mentoring as a 'vertical' process whereby young people learn how to 'be' in society. Bly's argument is that the breakdown of vertical relationships has created a sibling society where members of society live out a perpetual adolescence. This, he agues, can be seen in organizations where employees find it difficult to accept more responsibility for themselves and the organization. Outside work organizations mentoring has broad social implications for our society in how we develop the vulnerable and young. Mentors and their wisdom, therefore, have the potential to tackle many issues facing us today.

Believing in your wisdom

Another issue mentors need to be aware of is something called 'the imposter syndrome'. This is when a person believes they are less competent than others and that their previous achievements were down to luck or the team they worked with. They fear that at any moment they will be discovered as a fraud. What we are talking about here is not a genuine incompetence but rather a limiting belief, and it is particularly prevalent in high-achieving women. It can be resolved with a good mentor who can reconcile the discrepancy between a person's achievements and their perceived ability. Change of any kind is difficult and a good mentor understands this.

Why change is so difficult

Can you recall when what you have learned hindered learning something new?

- The experience of driving on the wrong side of the road in a different country?
- Having the hot and cold taps reversed in a house?
- Falling into the same behaviour pattern even though determined to change it?

Then you will know how hard change is. Today we are bombarded with thousands of bits of data at any time. For our brains to cope they are programmed to process information as efficiently as possible, with minimum thought and attention. But this has the side-effect of making change difficult. Most of the time behaviour, including thinking, is on automatic pilot. Have you experienced driving home and realize you've been unaware of part of the journey? Our brains quickly move actions or thought patterns that are frequently repeated to non-consciousness. The brain seizes incoming data it recognizes and classifies it, activating the most relevant category or 'schema'.

Sometimes we experience a situation that is not easy to classify, that seems new to us, or that requires complex or innovative thinking like a new project or way of working. In this situation, our 'working memory' is engaged, rapidly cataloguing and classifying it, matching it against previous experiences, ready to layer meaning to it.

Different parts of the brain handle these distinct ways of processing information. The 'automatic' brain processing area, the basal ganglia, requires little energy, has vast capacity, runs under our radar and allows us to be very efficient. Humans are 'cognitive misers', neurally programmed to maximize routine responses and operate mostly from our assumptions and expectations. Most of the time this is very effective – until we have to deal with something new.

The prefrontal cortex, or working memory, is involved in processing new or complex information. It has limited capacity, is energy intensive, is easily depleted and requires focused attention. Using the prefrontal cortex feels like hard word to most people. They may feel very hungry and even complain that it hurts their heads to think. This is because when we are utilizing the prefrontal cortex, focusing our attention, we are actually forging new neural circuits. Focusing our attention actually changes our brain structures and processes, making new ways of thinking and behaving more likely. But attention must be focused and sustained for a period of time to create those brain changes.

So thinking and behaviour changes really depend upon our focus of attention, be this:

- on work problems and solutions;
- on our enjoyment or dislike of work tasks;
- on our strengths and weaknesses.

Mentoring is a great opportunity for this sort of focus. Personality and behaviour are different and should not be confused. Fundamental is to realize that behaviours can change for the better when focused. The result is new insight, and new insights can be fleeting or long lasting depending upon continuing practice of the new thought or action. The insights become new neural circuits, 'institutionalized' by focusing attention. Contrast this with flashes of insight from a training programme that never translates into thinking or behaviour change.

These neural processes also illustrate ways we learn best and most enduringly. For example, when people solve a problem themselves instead of being told by their boss, the brain releases a rush of neurotransmitters like adrenaline. This burst of energy can be motivational, helping people think and behave differently.

Addressing the gap

Mentoring has the ability to address and resolve the gap between our power and our wisdom. It can bring long-lasting change in our thinking and behaviour and help overcome the thinking that prevents us performing to the best of our ability.

REFLECTIVE ACTION

- How can you incorporate a discussion on wisdom with mentors?
- How would mentees benefit from developing wisdom?
- How can you establish whether mentors have an open mindset?
- How will you evaluate changes in behaviour in mentees?

Chapter Eight
Mentoring for small and medium enterprises

While mentoring in large corporate organizations is growing, there is a need for quality mentoring for small to medium business owners. What entrepreneurs say they require are mentors who have built a successful business and who, in addition, understand the role and have the skills to be an effective mentor. The UK government made this announcement on 11 November 2010:

> A network of business mentors is to be established to provide new firms with valuable support and advice. The government sees mentoring as an important way of sharing both expertise and enthusiasm among the UK's entrepreneurial community.
>
> (*Financial Times*, 2010)

The annual Small Business Survey for 2007/08 found that businesses that used external advice were twice as likely to have increased the size of their workforce and to be planning business growth over the next three years than those that had not used advice. To make it easier for people to get the mentoring help they need, the government is planning a single network of some 40,000 entrepreneurs whose knowledge and skills can be tapped into by aspiring business people. The network will not only help start-ups but also growing firms and businesses seeking financial advice.

Announcing the network, Vince Cable, the Business Secretary, said:

> The best people to advise new entrepreneurs and existing businesses are those who have already started and run successful companies. Mentoring is a very effective way of promoting start-ups, higher productivity and growth amongst established businesses, so I am delighted to announce this new network. I also want to encourage more businesses to sign up and offer their support and guidance. We need as many successful mentors as possible to guide the next generation of entrepreneurs and businesses.
>
> (*Financial Times*, 2010)

Mark Prisk, the Business and Enterprise Minister, added:

> In the current economic climate, it has never been more important to promote an enterprise culture in the UK, and mentors play a crucial role in advising, supporting and encouraging entrepreneurs and small businesses. This new mentoring network will be invaluable for businesses all over the country. The network should be up and running from summer 2011 and will provide a single online gateway to mentoring provision.
>
> (*Financial Times*, 2010)

However, none of this has been based on what SMEs need or how they prefer to receive that help. Last year I was commissioned to find out and therefore it is very relevant to include mentoring for SMEs in this book to help them too. In fact, if the economy in the UK is to improve, the need to support established, growing SMEs is paramount as they are the companies that will be able to offer employment and improve export revenue.

One of the key factors that came out of the research was the importance of how business owners choose where to go for advice. For example, one 35-year-old said he went to his accountant and bank manager because they were the same age as him, and he felt they had common interests, upon which they had built a relationship. Another business owner said trust was key in deciding where he went for advice. This is reiterated by the studies Kevin Mole has made at Warwick University; he stated in a conversation we had that a trusting relationship is vital for how business owners choose advice.

At one focus group I ran, the business owners said the key was finding the right person with experience of running a business who also had access to a network that would be useful to tap into. One participant said 'It came under the heading of strategic review that ran as a series of four or five workshops. What made it effective was the way it was facilitated – asking the right questions.' They all agreed the key was having continual assistance over time at different growth stages. There is no doubt that at each growth stage a business has to deal with more risk and more challenges, whether a skills gap or ensuring the right strategy and markets. The chairman of a 16-year-old company remarked 'The advice gave the company new impetus and help to galvanise the team in moving to the next level.' The managing director of a 10-year-old company remarked 'It was very good support that allowed us to grow.' They added this did not necessarily mean support from retired people and that it needed to be more than what they could gain from the Institute of Directors and the Federation of Small Businesses.

These demonstrate the need for business advice to be available at different times in the life of a business. It is also worth pointing out that anyone watching the TV programme *Dragon's Den* realizes that those participating on the programme with their business ideas look for business advice and experience from the 'dragons' as much as funding. Having a network that provided advice was an important issue for those who were more likely to be growing their business in this study.

In Ostgaard and Birley's (1996) study they found a positive link between networking and company growth. In Germany, Bruderl and Preisendorfer (1998) found that business owners who had a broad social network were more successful. This was also confirmed in a UK study by Pickernell *et al* (2008), who stated 'having a wider range of sources of advice, and a greater number of types of advice are positively related to having higher growth orientations/aspirations.'

In 2010, similar remarks were echoed by the business owners of companies in my own research. One director said 'Some networks are good for sharing similar problems with similar people; other networks are good for generating new business.' Therefore, networks are important to growing businesses for different reasons.

The chief executive of an 11-year-old company said:

> It was a really positive experience. We were fortunate to have been given the opportunity to work with some great people offering advice of a very high standard. Their enthusiasm for our company was encouraging and their professional approach gave us the confidence to meet the challenges ahead.

Therefore, a network that provides mentoring specifically for SMEs would enhance our economic growth.

In my research, the most preferred way of delivering business support was workshops at 73 per cent, with short seminars second choice at 60 per cent. The third choice was to have face-to-face sessions with an adviser or mentor. Workshops and face-to-face provision can include having time to reflect. In studies on how entrepreneurs learn, Cope (2001) demonstrates that learning takes place through having time to reflect on experience. Additional literature supports this (Cope, 2005; Corbett, 2005; Clarke *et al*, 2006). Business mentors will have mixed experiences, so matching will be important because every business is different and has different needs, as shown by the answers to the question of what a business mentor could help with:

> New ideas and strategy.
>
> Strategy and the impact of the recession – how we can amend it for the next five years.

Help with personnel – we need to find qualified people. We also need legal help and specialist marketing in branding.

Operational. Our product and sales are good but we need day-to-day operational help.

Sales training.

It was through recent management training we realized we have holes in our structure and marketing. So help with these.

R&D product development, marketing and help with finding new markets.

The Government is keen to provide mentors for new businesses but it is the growing, established businesses that also need mentors. When asked when is the most crucial time in the life of the business for support and advice, business owners were clear:

At all times, particularly during change. This is when it's most valued.

All the way through the life of a business. An annual health check with a six-monthly strategic review would make a real difference.

During growth and with an HR consultant.

We've grown organically so we've never had a loan but some practical input on how we run the business would be useful.

The situation always changes so different help at different times. In the first year you make mistakes, the second year is OK, then the third you go through growth.

We are OK at sorting out the difficult times such as recession but where support is needed is in times of growth.

The knowledge and experiences of mentors for business owners will be complex. When asked what sort of support they will need in the future, business owners each had their own needs:

Support for manufacturing as it's difficult to compete globally.

Transitional – we are going to be moving to a larger business and increasing eight- to tenfold. We will need a programme for exporting, seeking advice on tax, shipping, import/exporting and manufacturing.

Help with improving the processes for tendering, particularly at local council level.

They were asked, what are you looking for in the relationship with an adviser or mentor?

Empathy. You get more productive help if they have experience.

Someone with experience and credibility. Most consultants don't understand.

It's down to the individual. I've just changed banks for that reason and now we have an excellent service.

We interviewed three people to help us and chose a 'school headmaster' type of guy. We are young and wanted experience. Then afterwards he handed us over to someone geographically closer who is very good.

Someone who has been and done it, and will not lecture you.

It was found in this study that the intention of business owners was also a factor in how established businesses grow and this is something mentors will need to build on. Business drivers such as the aspirations, ambition, resilience and motivation of business owners are important. While these elements are not prevalent in some of the academic research papers, they came out in the one-to-one interviews undertaken in the study. For example, one of the business owners was a young man who started on the shop floor, bought the business two-and-a-half years ago and today employs 50 people. He remarked that his aspiration was to own the business he was working for and when he needed external advice he found it. 'Business Link helped me implement the strategy and were a sounding board when things felt a bit lonely.' He added: 'I couldn't have expanded as fast without them.'

Therefore, the intentions of the business owners should be considered. Bird (1988) states that:

The founder's intentions determine the form and direction of an organization at its inception. Subsequent organizational success, development (including written plans), growth and change are based on these intentions, which are either modified, elaborated, embodied or transformed.

In a study of businesses belonging to the Federation of Small Businesses, Pickernell *et al* (2003) support the above by saying 'Understanding growth intentions are therefore important as these aspirations play a critical function in the actual growth by firms'. Businesses have to deal with the unexpected and so sometimes a business owner has to be open to intentions at an unexpected time. Mole told me that businesses must be 'ready' for support and that this can come at different times. An example from my own study explains this. After 15 years in business the owner died following the discovery of cancer seven weeks earlier. His wife had a financial background and decided to run the business herself. She relied on her management team and outside networks and mentors. Today the business has come through the recession with no redundancies and her son is now working alongside her. She is growing the business at this difficult economic time and recruiting more people. Her intention is to carry on building what her husband began.

Warren Bennis says:

> All organizations, especially those that are growing, walk a tightrope between stability and change, tradition and revision. Therefore, they must have some means of reflecting on their own experiences and offering reflective structures for their employees.
>
> (Bennis, 2003)

Intention and resilience are vital, but having business support at different times based on trusting relationships is what enables these growing companies to continue to grow, even in times of recession. As someone who advises on mentoring schemes I believe that any national scheme for SMEs will need to find people who:

- are willing to help people grow and develop;
- demonstrate leadership;
- have credibility with their peers and those they will be mentoring;
- show they are people-centred;
- have strong interpersonal skills, especially empathy;
- take responsibility;
- be good communicators;
- know how to use personal power and influence to get things done;
- be a positive role model.

There will be some people who will have these qualities, but care needs to be taken, as being successful with one business does not necessarily mean the same experience will work with others. Each business is very different and has different needs. The development of the mentors will be fundamental, as going into another business and telling the owner what to do because it worked for you is not mentoring. Therefore, caution is required.

CASE STUDY   Hansen Glass

During the late 1990s, Hansen Glass, based in Liverpool, had a new managing director, Stewart Barnes. It was then a £6 million pound company and was loss-making. Stewart implemented a new business strategy and at its core he envisioned empowered teams. A new structure with team leaders was created with some staff becoming appointed 'managers' for the first time. To support these people, Stewart and his newly created senior management team agreed, created and implemented a mentoring scheme with the assistance of Leyland Trucks, which had developed an excellent mentoring scheme and were now assisting SMEs to do the same.

The top team were to mentor the new managers. They used the advice from Leyland Trucks to produce a 12-page booklet that included the role of a mentor, the role of a mentee, how mentoring differs from coaching and what to do to enable a mentoring scheme to work. This was put into the context of Hansen Glass and a contract was developed on how the scheme would work. It was agreed that the mentor and mentee would meet once a month for an hour over a two-year period. First, the mentors practised on each other to gain confidence, then each member of the top team mentored a team leader to support them in the challenging, unionized environment.

I asked Stewart and the current managing director, Ian Whalley, who was one of the senior managers Stewart employed, about the outcomes from the scheme they had put in place:

> It was great to see the mentees taking on more responsibility and moving from an operational role to managing not only in Liverpool but also in a new site many miles away. We were delighted that the team leaders 'stepped up' not only to do what we expected they could do but also to drive continuous improvement and the performance of the business. This enabled senior managers to spend more time on the more strategic aspects of developing the organization. At the same time, being a mentor has developed our people skills and our knowledge of when to deploy mentoring.

One of the mentees was Bill Wilcock and he described the experience from his perspective:

> I was a team leader at the time. Stewart linked us up with directors and I was teamed up with Stewart, which was really enlightening as I saw what the managing director of a company gets up to. During the mentoring meetings we tackled tasks, problems, people issues, what could be done and tools that could eliminate some problems. I felt encouraged because it knocked down the walls of the hierarchy and I wasn't just one individual in the corner of the company. Since then I've studied lots of management topics and Japanese manufacturing methodologies. It gives you confidence that you lack if you don't have the tools. It means you are not shifting 'widgets' but achieving results through people and encouraging them.

Today, with quite a flat structure in the UK, Ian Whalley is mentoring a Hansen Group team in Denmark while Stewart is now a non-executive director of a £20 million company that has been recognized as the fastest growing manufacturing company in the UK. Here, he is using the essence of the Hansen Glass mentoring programme with his new board to develop aspiring managers to improve upon the already impressive track record.

Finding your mentor

Each growth stage of your business will have different and more complex challenges. The success of Carphone Warehouse in the UK included good mentoring, yet finding the right person isn't easy for business owners. But like other objectives you have to make it a priority and it is then more likely to happen. You need to find someone who really understands what you are doing, respects you for it and who you feel you can trust. The choice is different from that of a corporate employee – this is your business, your ideas and innovation, your money and your risks.

The best way is to ask people – your bank manager, accountant, family, friends or other business owners. However, you don't want someone who is only good with spreadsheets; ideally, find someone who has experience in your field – someone who can both advise and provide useful connections. Many successful entrepreneurs want to share their knowledge with others. What is important is that you are clear about what you want to achieve from the mentoring experience. The rest is not so different from what has been covered so far in the book.

Words of wisdom

Today, SMEs have two main issues that they are having to fight on both fronts: the banks are reluctanct to lend, while at the same time the media is creating a loss of confidence in business. I end this chapter with a different view, from a successful businessman.

The words below are from someone who knows the problems all too well. He has run small and large companies and was at the heart of banking supervision before the recent 'crash'. He is a wise mentor who admits his mistakes as keenly as the rest of us and learns from them. Today, he mentors business people and so it is appropriate to capture his words here for business owners to reflect on.

We have to deal with the uncomfortable truth that, collectively, our generation screwed up. The institutions of the state didn't shout 'stop', including the regulator and its board, of which I was chair. In the early years we didn't ask enough of the right questions, we didn't sufficiently pursue the questions we did ask and so we were blind to the risks.

Generally, our generation took on too much household debt; businesses became over-extended; we allowed ourselves to be lured into the property market; believed we were 'masters of the universe' with little to learn; believed over-exuberant economic growth was our birthright and would continue regardless of the fundamental laws of economics; we lost control of ourselves; elected governments who told us it would never end. In one way or another we all screwed up!

The net result is we are in deep trouble. Businesses are starved of cash, households are struggling and the vulnerable are afraid – with society seeming to be pulling apart at the seams.

How do we pull back?

Business owners know that confidence is at the heart of economic activity and that it's in short supply and draining away at the present time. This is made worse by the media, commentators and politicians who just want to make a name for themselves. If we spook the markets, confidence will take another dive, like a self-fulfilling prophecy. Doom mongers do great damage to countries because they destroy the confidence that is at the heart of any economy. The media and politicians have led an orgy of blame, scapegoating, negativity and pessimism.

But this is not the end of the world. Business owners are still vital, energetic and creative people. We have a vibrant culture from music to theatre to art. We need positive thoughts and actions.

It's been found that people who are unrealistically optimistic:

- perform better;
- have more fulfilled relationships;
- are happier.

Whereas people who are realistic:

- are overwhelmed by problems before they start;
- perform worse.

So yes, we have serious problems and challenges – and we mustn't make light of this. Yes, many people are in financial trouble. Yes, many businesses are struggling to survive. But we have to believe we can get out of this.

It's no good 'calling on government'. We have to do this ourselves. We need business people to step up and lead. There are three things we can do:

1 Let's get this into perspective:
   - remember how much we've got going for us;
   - we've been here before, in 1987 when unemployment was higher and the standard of living lower, and we pulled out of it.

2 Recover self-confidence:
   - start believing in ourselves as business people again;
   - stay away from negative people – be it politicians, commentators, the media or anyone!
   - avoid those commentators who have never run a business or couldn't manage their way out of a paper bag!

3 Believe we can work our way out of this:
   - because our generation simply has to fix this;
   - believe we will emerge from this;
   - learn some deep lessons from it;
   - be more disciplined;
   - generate better values to live and work by;
   - develop a better country for our children and grandchildren.

There is no doubt that the next couple of years will be tough and having access to a mentor who can specifically help SMEs will be vitally important. However, business owners learn from others but are not made by others. This is a journey they take themselves. But along that journey they will find mentors who will guide and inspire them. They may not be part of a formal mentoring system as in a large organization, but they will be there.

What appears to be crucial for business owners is to stay positive – even when things are difficult. What we know from the writers on positive psychology is that it is more productive to strengthen strengths than to strengthen weaknesses. This is the role of a mentor for business owners – to not skim over the realities but to help the mentee keep a positive mindset. By doing so, employees in the business are more likely to be creative, innovative, and committed to it.

Jim Collins, author of *Good to Great* (2001; a 'must read' for business owners) spends his spare time rock climbing, which has enabled him to see an important analogy. He says: 'Breakthroughs come not primarily by changing what we do, but by changing first and foremost how we think about what we do. And that is the toughest climb of all.' (Collins, 2003).

REFLECTIVE ACTION

- What actions can you take to find a mentor for yourself?
- What can you do to stay positive?

Chapter Nine
Mentoring for leadership

Like mentoring, leadership as a concept has been around a long time. In fact, the concept of leadership is much older. It can be found in the earliest Egyptian hieroglyphics and ancient Chinese writings. For the last 50 years psychologists, political scientists and more recently business academics have studied and tried to teach leadership. The truth is that, generally, it hasn't worked. There are many reasons for this, some of which will be explored here. Can mentoring do any better?

The challenge

The media reports daily on the failure of the current generation of leaders to guide their organizations in a world characterized by constantly accelerating change. For over a decade organizations across the UK in the public and private sectors have spent millions trying to develop leadership. Why? It is widely recognized that effective leadership is fundamental, especially when change or transformation is required. Yet most leadership training or courses fail to have a lasting impact on the leadership behaviour of their participants.

In 2008 Kaisen psychologists concluded that British businesses alone were wasting £75 million a year on leadership development programmes for managers. They interviewed 10,000 leaders from 27 companies, of which 20 companies were in the FTSE 250. They said 'Most of the methods used on these programmes focused on educating leaders by giving them useful concepts and theories.' However, the report indicated that the capabilities programmes were trying to develop, such as leadership and motivational skills, were not being transferred in this way.

Similar research at the Said Business School in Oxford also came to the same conclusion. This study included courses offered by Warwick, Cranfield and Henley, and concluded they did not offer value. It included interviews with 60 senior HR people who had sent individuals to the courses as well as 90 executives who had attended the programmes.

The study also indicated that purchasers found it difficult to judge the quality of consultants and training providers, yet at the same time found internal programmes did not produce the leadership results they desired. This is a serious problem, because most organizations reported a shortage of future leaders, not enough to carry out their mission-critical strategies. Therefore identifying and conducting high-impact leadership development programmes is a crucial concern for UK organizations.

One common reason for the lack of effective leadership development is usually that senior management doesn't fully support the programmes. Research found that one of the reasons for lack of support was that senior executives know intuitively that leadership is not about competency frameworks or training programmes. Their personal experience has shown them that leadership is learned in practice.

It seems that Distinguished Professor Warren Bennis of the University of Southern California is right when he says:

> Leaders are not made by corporate courses, any more than they are made by their college courses, but by experience. Therefore, it is not devices, such as 'career path planning,' or training courses, that are needed, but an organization's commitment to providing its

potential leaders with opportunities to learn through experience in an environment that permits growth and change.

(Bennis, 2003)

Enabling effective mentoring for leadership development

Mentoring is one way to help people reflect and learn from their leadership experiences. However, mentors whose focus is on developing leadership need to have developed their own leadership capability and understand the complexity of leadership. They also need to be aware of some of the newest understandings of the concept, including implicit leadership theories, leadership identity and leadership self-efficacy. These new areas are only touched on here but at the Institute of Leadership we develop mentors who are wise to all the new work around leadership and most importantly how people actually learn leadership.

When people attend a leadership programme they already have an understanding of leadership that has developed from childhood. In other words, everyone will have an implicit leadership theory – beliefs about leadership as a concept, whether they regard themselves as a leader and why or why not. Implicit leadership theories (ILTs) are culturally shared but include some assumptions about leadership held in common by people around the world. They influence our responses to authority figures, whether we identify with the concept, whether we feel confident to express leadership or put ourselves forward for a leadership role, and how we express that leadership.

In my own research with young people, ILTs were found in most children aged 5 and upwards. They had a view of what leadership should be and differentiated between a leader and leadership. For young people at school it was found that the prototype leader was 'bossy, big, controlling, used power, was more intelligent or more talented than others' (Owen, 2007). People then carry this implicit theory in their heads and if they think 'I'm not like that, so I'm not a leader' they may disassociate themselves from the label 'leader'. While the media and teachers influence this, the strongest influence with young people is a parent. It was also found that gender, school year and type of school affected children's self-identification as leaders and this tends to stay with individuals, though how they respond to it differs.

Early on in a career a boss can influence ILTs. For example, one woman we worked with had come from banking and on joining was told by the bank manager that she could forget going very far in her career, as women were not leaders. This stayed with her for years, limiting her identity as a leader and her career overall. For other women, this attempt to limit someone's career would make them even more determined to succeed. My research showed that both teachers and managers apparently limit the pool of potential leaders based on their own implicit leadership prototype. Therefore, a leadership mentor needs to know how to recognize and deal with this.

Unlearning implicit leadership theories

Unlearning is 'the process of reducing or eliminating pre-existing knowledge or habits that would otherwise represent formidable barriers to new learning' (Newstrom, 1983). In the film *The Empire Strikes Back* Yoda is mentoring young Luke Skywalker. He says 'You have to unlearn what you have learned', and this is an important part of mentoring for leadership.

Unlearning is key to changing limiting aspects of implicit leadership theories, particularly narrow leadership prototypes (such as 'bossy') and non-leaders identity ('I'm not bossy so I'm not a leader'). Therefore understanding the process of unlearning should be part of a mentor's development, to enable them to know the different ways of achieving this. Another limiting aspect for mentees is something called 'attachment security'.

Attachment security and leadership mentoring

Attachment security is based on our early relationship with caregivers, usually parents. It's relevant to leadership because it is linked to many interpersonal skills and attitudes required for leadership. At the Institute of Leadership, my colleague Dr Tracey Manning has been sharing her work in this field to help develop leadership in others. Her work has found that more confident, socially competent, secure people can demonstrate more group or team leadership and transformational leadership. Secure attachment predicts greater trust, emotional intelligence, work satisfaction, ability to delegate, and having less work/ family conflict as well as practise leadership.

Insecure individuals develop fewer interpersonal skills and have more difficulty with relationships – work and personal. Insecure attachment can result in workaholism, micro-management and difficult relationships with line managers. Through reflection as part of mentoring, mentors can help identify and change the negative assumptions about themselves and others. This is quite a challenge for mentors and shows how important their develop-ment is to understand these issues.

Another area where mentors can be extremely effective is in building self-efficacy in mentees.

Mentoring and leadership self-efficacy

In his study on self-efficacy, Professor of Psychology Albert Bandura reviewed nearly two thousand published studies examining the role of self-efficacy and found beliefs about personal capabilities affected academic achievement, athletic performance, career choice, decision making, stress tolerance, teaching performance and voter participation. In other words, confidence in one's task-specific abilities has been determined to be an important causal variable for understanding and improving performance in achievement settings. He defines self-efficacy as the 'belief in one's capabilities to organize and execute the courses of action required to produce given attainments' (Bandura, 1997).

Findings have linked self-efficacy with whether a person experiences self-hindering or self-aiding thought patterns, how much effort they will exert on a given task and how long they will persist in the face of difficulties. This means that individuals with high self-efficacy are motivated, persistent, goal-directed, resilient and clear thinkers under pressure. Self-efficacy is highly domain specific, which means that it can be unique and specific for certain tasks. Leadership self-efficacy determines how leaders behave, think and become motivated to be involved with particular roles. It refers to feeling confident in a leadership situation or in one's general ability to lead. As a leader develops greater levels of self-efficacy, motivation to complete the specific task also increases. It has also been shown through different studies recently that leader self-efficacy beliefs contribute to leadership performance and it is this relationship specifically that I would like to focus on.

Those with higher leadership self-efficacy:

- challenge and motivate themselves and others;
- persist towards goals in the face of obstacles;

- build group and team confidence and their teams are more likely to reach their goals.

Strengthening people's confidence in their leadership capabilities empowers them to take on leadership initiatives and roles while benefiting from leadership learning. Therefore, developmental experiences, combined with reflection and constructive feedback from a mentor will result in greater self-efficacy.

Self-confidence is an important part of effective leadership and was the most cited reason for not practising leadership in my research with young people up to age 18. However, self-confidence and self-efficacy are not identical concepts. Self-confidence is a general sense of capability that is often considered as a personal trait and one that teachers look for in young people to practise leadership. As a personal trait it is not subject to change. In contrast, self-efficacy is a personal belief, a self-judgement about having the capabilities for one specific task. This is more a cognitive process and therefore is subject to change if given the appropriate conditions. The two may be different in concept but they are related even though, according to self-efficacy theory, it is the individual's belief regarding their capabilities to successfully perform the leadership task that is the causal factor. In other words, it is self-efficacy not self-confidence. Likewise, self-esteem is different from self-efficacy and Bandura explains the difference thus: 'Perceived self-efficacy is concerned with judgements of personal capability, whereas self-esteem is concerned with judgements of self-worth.' He adds that: 'People need much more than high self-esteem to do well in given pursuits' (Bandura, 1997).

In 2000 Chemers *et al* concluded that leadership self-efficacy 'clearly contributes to leadership effectiveness'. In addition, there is a positive relationship between leadership self-efficacy and the willingness to take on a leadership role. However, an individual with low leadership self-efficacy will avoid such experiences and therefore require a learning environment that is 'safe' and supportive to participate. Mentoring provides this environment and understanding the role self-efficacy plays and how developing self-efficacy gives mentors the capability to truly make a difference to individuals, including their leadership capabilities.

In addition, mentoring that develops self-enhancing attributions builds self-efficacy and contributes to self-esteem. For example, 'Yes, I can take some credit for this success' is what the mentor is trying to help the mentee say. This isn't so easy in the UK as we sometimes accuse a person of being 'full of himself' or ask 'Who does she think she is?' So we tend to self-deprecate and beat ourselves up over disappointments, all of which limits self-efficacy and learning from experiences. This negative reaction also develops 'imposter syndrome' (believing one is less competent than others and attributing previous achievements and success to luck, the team or others).

The ongoing development of mentors is really important to understand and be able to deal with these barriers to leadership. For that reason, the recommendation in this book is that mentors have a structured development plan too.

Daniel Goleman, who popularized emotional intelligence, wrote about an organization he had been working with: 'When we assessed high level leaders at a large integrated-energy company, those we found to have a healthy repertoire of leadership strengths all told us the same story: They had first cultivated their strengths early in their careers, under the guardianship of a mentor' (Goleman, 2002). He went on to add that two chief executives had come from the mentoring scheme in the company.

Finding a good leadership mentor whose purpose is to give support and guidance is a crucial part of leadership development. They will understand that leadership is much more than job performance and includes self-awareness, understanding of and influencing others, being a master of the context you operate in, understanding the wider world, keeping positive even when things are tough and giving purpose to the work you do and the life you live.

Organizations grow leaders by helping individuals learn from experience and mentoring is a good way to do this. By using deep reflection with a mentor the mentee is able to have a better understanding of who they are; realize what matters to them, and how they can emerge stronger. Reflection through a mentor focuses judgement and transforms them in a fundamental way. When mentors do their work well they not only help the mentees to achieve their tasks successfully, but also enable them to see the broader context that gives their work meaning.

Finally, the role of mentee at the end of the mentoring process is not only to make better decisions but also to strive continuously to develop leadership in others. So the circle of organizational life continues.

REFLECTIVE ACTION

- What does leadership mean to you? What is your implicit leadership theory?

- How confident do you feel in leading this project of setting up a mentoring scheme?

- Who is your mentor?

Chapter Ten
Conclusion

This manual isn't a large, academic book. The aim was to produce a practical guide for those interested in mentoring and wanting to set up a mentoring scheme or wanting to improve the mentoring scheme they have. In this concluding chapter it helps to pull together the three keys areas requiring focus for a successful mentoring scheme.

1 Preparation

It is vital to carry out a proper process in order to set up an excellent mentoring scheme within an organization. To ensure this, ask these questions:

- What is the purpose of the mentoring scheme? What are you trying to achieve?

- Is your organization ready in the long term to invest in this? Do you have support (in actions not just words) from the top of the organization?

- What do you aim to achieve? What are the outcomes in measurable terms?

- How are you going to evaluate and measure the impact? What is the evaluation plan?

- Who is going to administer the mentoring scheme (this is not necessarily HR and is a great project for an up and coming 'star')? What credibility do they have within the organization? Can they get through gate-keepers and communicate with the top? What development do they need?

- What is the communication plan that will ensure everyone knows about the scheme? What materials are you going to use to support this? Are these materials ready?

- What is the structure and what are the procedures? How will you identify, select and develop mentors? What are the reporting strategies for this?

- Who will be the first mentees? Will you run a pilot?

- How often will you review and improve the scheme?

2 Ongoing development of mentors

In all the case studies the same message came from mentors. 'I get as much out of the sessions as the mentee. We are learning together.' Mentors want to learn and share their learning in the role of mentor. Therefore it is vital to have regular development for active mentors. These are usually half a day to a day every four to six months. It's clear from the manual that there is much to learn and these sessions keep mentors motivated and are often fun.

3 Supporting the administration team

Both mentors and mentees need to know who is in the administration team, and that they can be communicated with at any time. Likewise the administration team need to communicate with mentors and mentees to establish progress, deal with any difficulties and keep communicating the benefits of the scheme across the organization. Where schemes fall down is failure in this area. It's not enough to launch the scheme with a big bang and then expect everyone to engage. The communication plan is an ongoing process.

So many schemes fail because once launched their development is left to chance. To help, the Institute of Leadership has a mentoring resource kit to aid organizations. It also provides some interesting half-day and day 'master classes' for mentors to continue their development to becoming a great mentor.

The big picture

At the beginning of the book there was a warning that if we do not address the gap between our power and our wisdom our future would be bleak. It was James Mcgregor Burns (1979) who wrote 'We all have power to do acts we lack the motive to do... We all have the motives to do things we do not have the resources to do'. For him motive and resources were essential for power. If we give someone the resource of a mentor with motive to change things for the better – whether it is with their team, their organization or their country – they have an opportunity to use their power for a purpose. Power has both a negative and a positive side to it. In recent years we have seen too much of the negative side of power. It's now time to flip it over and see the positive side.

It was Athena, goddess of wisdom, who enabled her mentee, Telemachus, to use wisdom and with it strength to beat the invaders. Today, our 'invaders' may look different but they are there whether its greed and ego or aggressive competitors. Good mentoring can help plug the gap between power and wisdom for a fast-changing world.

The overthrow of dictators is spreading across the world, but with it large gaps are appearing that are dangerous if filled with more self-interested power-grabbers or those who kowtow to wealthy nations for money that ends up in the pockets of the few. A few good men and women who can act as mentors are needed now.

Whether in schools, companies, government departments or across the world, mentoring to close the gap between power and wisdom is required on a global scale. This is why having the right mentors and continually developing them is so important. We each can contribute to the 'big picture'.

In the last analysis, the essential thing is the life of the individual. This alone makes history, here alone do the great transformations just take place, and the whole future, the whole history of the world, ultimately springs as a gigantic summation from these hidden sources in individuals. In our most private and most subjective lives we are not only the passive witnesses of our age, and its sufferers, but also its makers. We make our own epoch.

(Jung)

REFLECTIVE ACTION

- What are the first steps you are now going to take?

References

Alvesson, M and Willmott, H (1992) On the idea of emancipation in management and organization studies, *Academy of Management Review*, **17** (3), pp 432–464

Ardelt, M (2005) Wisdom as expert knowledge system: A critical review of a contemporary operationalization of an ancient concept, *Human Development*, **47**, pp 257–285

Argyris, C and Schon, D (1996) *Organisational Learning 11: Theory, Method and Practice*, Addison-Wesley

Bandura, A (1997) *Self-Efficacy: The Exercise of Control*, Freeman

Bennis, Warren (2003) *On Becoming a Leader* (revised edition), Basic Books

Bird (1988) Implementing entrepreneurial ideas: The case for intention, *Academy of Management Review*, **13**, pp 442–453

Bly, Robert (1996) *The Sibling Society*, Da Capo Press

Boorstin, DJ (1985) *The Discoverers*, Random House

Booze and Company (2008) *Strategy and Business*, **51**

Bpoud, D, Keogh, R and Walker, D (1985) *Turning Experience into Learning*, Kogan Page

Brockbank, A and McGill, I (1998) *Facilitating Reflective Learning in Higher Education*, SRHE, Open University Press

Bruderl, J and Preisendorfer, P (1998) Network support and the success of newly founded businesses, *Small Business Economics*, **10**, pp 213–225

Chemers, M M, Watson, C B and May, S (2000) Dispositional effect and leadership effectiveness, *Personality and Social Psychology Bulletin*, **26**

Clarke, J, Thorpe, R, Anderson, L and Gold, J (2006) It's all action, it's all learning: Action learning in SMEs, *Training*, **30**

Clutterbuck, D (1991) *Everyone Needs a Mentor*, 2nd edn, Pub Institute of Personnel and Development

Clutterbuck, D (1998) *Learning Alliances*, IPD

Collins, J (2001) *Good to Great*, Random House

Collins, J (2003) Leadership lessons from a rock climber, *Fast Company*, 1 December

Cope, J (2001) The entrepreneurial experience: Towards a dynamic learning perspective of entrepreneurship, unpublished PhD thesis, Lancaster University.

Cope, J (2003) Entrepreneurial learning and critical reflection: Discontinuous events as triggers for 'higher level' learning, *Management Learning*, **34** (4)

Cope, J (2005) Towards a dynamic learning perspective of entrepreneurship, *Entrepreneurship: Theory and Practice*, **29** (4)

Corbett, A C (2005) Experiential learning within the process of opportunity identification and exploitation, *Entrepreneurship: Theory and Practice*, **29** (4)

Dewey, J (1938) *Experience and Education*, Macmillan

Dweck, C (2006) *Mindset: The New Psychology of Success*, Random House

Early, A and Carla, L (2007) Leadership Labyrinth, *Harvard Business Review*, September

Financial Times 11 November 2010

Gluck, J and Bluck, S (2004) Making things better and learning a lesson: Experiencing wisdom across the lifespan, *Journal of Personality*, **72** (3), pp 543–572

Goleman, D (2002) *The New Leaders*, Little Brown

Gregerson, H B, Morrison, A J and Black, T S (1998) Developing leaders for the global frontier, *Sloan Management Review*, **40** (1), pp 21–433

Hay, J (1995) *Transformational Mentoring: Creating Development Alliances for Changing Organisational Cultures*, Sherwood Publishing

Honey, P and Mumford, A (1986) *The Manual of Learning Styles*, Maidenhead: Peter Honey Publications

House, R, Hanges, P, Dorfman, P, *et al* (1999) *The GLOBE Study*

Hoyt, C (2002) Women leaders: The role of stereotype activation of leadership self-efficacy, *Leadership Review*, Autumn

Isaacs, W (2000) Taking flight: Dialogue, collective thinking and organisational learning in strategic learning, in *Strategic Learning in A Knowledge Economy*, ed R Cross Jnr and S Israelit, Butterworth-Heinemann

Joplin, J and Daus, C (1997) Challenges of leading a diverse workforce, *The Academy of Management Education*, **11** (3), pp 32–48

Jung, C G (1934–1954) *The Archetypes and the Collective Unconscious*, Routledge and Kegan Paul

Kunzmann, U and Baltes, P B (2005) The psychology of wisdom: Theoretical and empirical challenges, in *Handbook of Wisdom: Psychological Perspectives*, ed R J Sternberg and J Jordan, Cambridge University Press, pp 110–135

McGregor Burns, J (1979) *Leadership*, Harper and Row

McKee, P and Barber, C (1999) On defining wisdom, *International Journal of Aging and Human Development*, **49**, pp 149–164

Moreton-Cooper, A and Palmer, A (2000) *Mentoring and Preceptorship*, Blackwell Science

Newstrom, J W (1983) The management of unlearning: Exploding the 'clean slate' fallacy, *Training and Development Journal*, 37 (8), p 36

Ostgaard, T and Birley, S (1996) New venture growth and personal networks, *Journal of Business Research*, **36** (1), pp 37–50

Owen, H (2007) *Creating Leaders in the Classroom*, Routledge

Pasupathi, M and Staudinger, U M (2001) Do advanced moral reasoners also show wisdom? Linking moral reasoning and wisdom-related knowledge and judgement, *International Journal of Behavioural Development*, **25**, pp 401–415

Pickernell, D, Peckham, G, Miller, C, *et al* (2008) *Strategies for Small Business Development and Growth. The Roles and Importance of Formal and Informal Sources of Business Support in Young Firms: Evidence from the UK's 2008 Federation of Small Business Survey*

Report by Kaisen Psychologists 2008

Roberts, A (1999) Homer's mentor: Duties fulfilled or misconstrued? *History of Education Journal*, November, pp 81–90

Roberts, A (2000) Mentoring revisited: A phenomenological reading of the literature, *Mentoring and Tutoring*, 8 (2), pp 145–170

Roche, G R (1979) Probing opinions, *Harvard Business Review*, 57 (1), p 15

Senge, P (1990) *The Fifth Discipline*, Doubleday

Senge, P, Scharmer, O, Jaworski, J *et al* (2005) *Presence*, Nicholas Brealey

Sorum Brown, J (2006) Reflective practices for transformational leaders, *Future Age*, May/June

Thomson, P (2010) *Financial Times*, 13 October

Wheatley, M (2002) *Turning to One Another: Simple Conversations to Restore Hope to the Future*, Berrett-Koeller

Appendix
Learning styles

Learning styles questionnaire

There are no right or wrong answers and it is best to answer as quickly as you can as honestly as possible, rather than giving what you think the answer should be. If you agree more than disagree with a statement, put a tick next to it. If you disagree more than agree, put a cross. Make sure you put a tick or cross next to every statement.

1 I have strong beliefs about what is right and what is wrong, good and bad.

2 I often act without considering the possible consequences.

3 I tend to solve problems using a step-by-step approach.

4 I believe that formal procedures and policies restrict people.

5 I have a reputation for saying what I think, simply and directly.

6 I often find that actions based on feelings are as sound as those based on careful thought and analysis.

7 I like the sort of work where I have time for thorough preparation and implementation.

8 I regularly question people about their basic assumptions.

9 What matters most is whether something works in practice.

10 I actually seek out new experiences.

11 When I hear about a new approach or idea I immediately start working out how to apply it in practice.

12 I am keen on self-discipline, such as watching my diet, taking regular exercise, sticking to a fixed routine, etc.

13 I take pride in doing a thorough job.

14 I get on best with logical, analytical people and less well with spontaneous, 'irrational' people.

15 I take over the interpretation of data available to me and avoid jumping to conclusions.

16 I like to reach a decision carefully after weighing up all the alternatives.

17 I am attracted more to novel, unusual ideas than to practical ones.

18 I don't like disorganisation and prefer to fit things into a coherent pattern.

19 I accept and stick to laid-down procedures and policies as long as I regard them as an efficient way of getting the job done.

20 I like to relate my actions to a general principle.

21 In discussions I like to get straight to the point.

22 I have to have distant, rather formal relationships with people at work.

23 I thrive on the challenge of tackling something new and different.

24 I enjoy fun-loving, spontaneous people.

25 I pay meticulous attention to detail before coming to a conclusion.

26 I find it difficult to produce ideas on impulse.

27 I believe in coming to the point immediately.

28 I am careful not to jump to conclusions too quickly.

29 I prefer to have as many sources of information as possible – the more data to think over the better.

30 Flippant people who don't take things seriously enough usually irritate me.

31 I listen to other people's points of view before putting my own forward.

32 I tend to be open about how I'm feeling.

33 In discussions I enjoy watching the manoeuvring of other participants.

34 I prefer to respond to events on a spontaneous, flexible basis rather than plan things out in advance.

35 I tend to be attracted to techniques such as network analysis, flow charts, branching programmes, contingency planning, etc.

36 It worries me if I have to rush out a piece of work to meet a tight deadline.

37 I tend to judge people's ideas on their practical merits.

38 Quiet, thoughtful people make me uneasy.

39 I often get irritated by people who want to rush things.

40 It is more important to enjoy the present moment than to think about the past or future.

41 I think that decisions made on a thorough analysis of all the information are sounder than those based on intuition.

42 I tend to be a perfectionist.

43 In discussions, I tend to put forward practical, realistic ideas.

44 In meetings I put forward practical, realistic ideas.

45 More often than not, rules are there to be broken.

46 I prefer to stand back from a situation and consider all the perspectives.

47 I can often see inconsistencies and weaknesses in other people's arguments.

48 On balance I talk more than I listen.

49 I can often see better, more practical ways to get things done.

50 I think written reports should be short and to the point.

51 I believe that rational, logical thinking should win the day.

52 I tend to discuss specific things with people rather than engaging in social discussion.

53 I like people who approach things realistically rather than theoretically.

54 In discussions, I get impatient with irrelevancies and digressions.

55 If I have a report to write I produce lots of drafts before settling on the final version.

56 I am keen to try things out to see if they work in practice.

57 I am keen to reach answers via a logical approach.

58 I enjoy being the one who talks a lot.

59 In discussions I often find I am a realist, keeping people to the point and avoiding wild speculations.

60 I like to ponder many alternatives before making up my mind.

61 In discussions with people I often find I am the most dispassionate and objective.

62 In discussions I am more likely to adopt a 'low profile' than to take the lead and do most of the talking.

63 I like to be able to relate current actions to a longer-term bigger picture.

64 When things go wrong I am happy to shrug them off and put it down to experience.

65 I tend to reject wild, spontaneous ideas as being impractical.

66 It's best to think carefully before taking action.

67 On balance I do the listening rather than the talking.

68 I tend to be tough on people who find it difficult to adopt a logical approach.

69 Most times I believe the ends justify the means.

70 I don't mind hurting other people's feelings so long as the job gets done.

71 I find the formality of having specific objectives and plans stifling.

72 I'm usually one of the people who put life into a party.

73 I do whatever is expedient to get the job done.

74 I quickly get bored with methodical, detailed work.

75 I am keen on exploring the basic assumptions, principles and theories underpinning things and events.

76 I'm always interested to find out what people think.

77 I like meetings to be run on methodical lines, sticking to a laid-down agenda, etc.

78 I steer clear of subjective or ambiguous topics.

79 I enjoy the drama and excitement of a crisis situation.

80 People often find me insensitive to their feelings.

(Honey and Mumford 1986)

Scoring

Score one point for each statement marked with a tick. No points are scored for those with a cross.

The numbers below relate to the number of each question. Mark a 1 next to those questions that you ticked. Add up each column, and the column with the highest number indicates your preferred learning style (see below for definitions).

2	7	1	5
4	13	3	9
6	15	8	11
10	16	12	19
17	25	14	21
23	28	18	27
24	29	20	35
32	31	22	37
34	33	26	44
38	36	30	49
40	39	42	50
43	41	47	53
45	46	51	54
48	52	57	56
58	55	61	59
64	60	63	65
71	62	68	69
72	66	75	70
74	67	77	73
79	76	78	80
Activist	Reflector	Theorist	Pragmatist

Learning descriptions

Activists

Activists involve themselves fully in new experiences. They enjoy the here and now and are happy to be dominated by immediate experiences. They are open-minded and enthusiastic about anything new. They revel in short-term crises and tackle problems by brainstorming. They thrive on challenges but are bored with implementation and long-term consolidation. They are gregarious and tend to seek out all activities around themselves.

Reflectors

Reflectors like to stand back and ponder experiences. They collect data and chew things over before coming to any conclusion. They tend to be cautious and thoughtful. They enjoy taking a back seat and observing people, listening, before making their own points. They often have an unruffled, easy air about them. When they act it is as part of a wide picture that includes the past as well as the present and others' observations as well as their own.

Theorists

Theorists adapt and integrate observations into complex but logical theories. They think problems through in a step-by-step way. They tend to be perfectionists who like things to fit into a rational scheme. They are keen on theories, models and principles and tend to be detached and analytical rather than subjective. They rigidly reject anything that does not fit with this mindset.

Pragmatists

Pragmatists are keen on trying new ideas, theories and techniques to see if they work in practice and take the first opportunity to experiment. They like to get on with things and act quickly and confidently on ideas that attract them. They hate 'beating around the bush' and can be impatient with ruminating. They want to see things happen in reality.

Learning through mentoring according to your learning style

If your preferred learning style is the *activist*, you will learn best from mentoring that provides:

- new experiences or opportunities;
- high visibility;
- being thrown in the deep end;
- generating new ideas with no constraints or structure.

If your preferred learning style is *reflector*, you will learn best from mentoring that involves:

- standing back and watching the mentor;
- using the mentoring sessions to think things through;
- providing a project that involves research or investigation;
- having the opportunity to review what has happened.

If your preferred learning style is the *theorist*, you will learn best from mentoring that involves:

- time to methodically explore interrelationships between ideas and situations;
- the chance to question and probe the methodology or assumptions behind something;
- being intellectually stretched;
- listening to ideas and concepts that emphasize logic or rationality.

If your preferred learning style is the *pragmatist*, you will learn best from mentoring where:

- there is an obvious link between the sessions and a problem or opportunity in your job;
- you can try out and practice new techniques with feedback;
- you are given opportunities to implement what you have learned;
- you can focus on practical issues.